# CELEBRITIES MY ARSE!

*Also by Ricky Tomlinson*

Ricky
Football My Arse!

# CELEBRITIES MY ARSE!

## Ricky Tomlinson

sphere

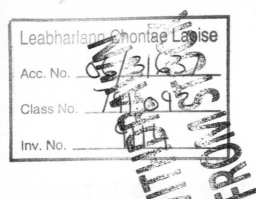
First published in Great Britain in 2006 by Sphere

Copyright © Ricky Tomlinson, Norman Giller 2006

The moral right of the authors has been asserted.

A CIP catalogue record for this book is available
from the British Library

ISBN-13: 978-0-316-02990-2
ISBN-10: 0-316-02990-4

Typeset in Melior and Akzidenz Grotesk by M Rules
Printed and bound in Great Britain by
Clays Ltd, St Ives plc

Sphere
An imprint of
Little, Brown Book Group
Brettenham House
Lancaster Place
London WC2E 7EN

A member of the Hachette Livre Group of Companies

www.littlebrown.co.uk

*To Rita and Eileen*
*Celebrity wives, my arse!*

# Contents

# Introduction
# by Jim Royle*

Ricky Tomlinson, a celebrity? My arse! His only claim to fame is that his gob's bigger than the mouth of the Mersey Tunnel.

Mind you, he deserves celebrity status ahead of those clowns who consider themselves stars just because they've made prats of themselves fox-trotting across our television screens, decorating a room with revolting wallpaper, spewing up in a jungle, or just rabbiting about nothing in a house full of boring strangers.

They call it reality TV. I call it smelly telly, because it stinks.

Celebrities, my arse!

Bloody hell's bells, next thing you know they'll be pointing a camera at some slob sitting in an armchair farting, scratching and pigging out on bacon butties. And they'll call him a celebrity.

I reluctantly have to admit that Tricky Ricky – or Rickety, as Ken Dodd calls him – has come up with a cracking collection of stories about REAL celebrities in this book.

As he's poked his nose (he usually picks it) into the lives and times of so many famous people in the following pages, I feel entitled to tell a tale out of school about him.

He was appearing as a guest on the BBC2 show *Petrolheads* in 2006, and had to park a motorised sofa while blindfolded. With his team captain Chris Barrie shouting directions, Ricky managed

---

*Jim Royle appears by kind permission of his creators Caroline Aherne and Craig Cash, who are *real* celebrities

to demolish the studio set that was designed to look like the lounge at my Royle home.

John Thomson, star of *Cold Feet* and *The Fast Show*, was next on the *Petrolheads* set, parking a Popemobile, again blindfolded. Ricky told the producers to prepare themselves for carnage, and sure enough John turned the Popemobile into a weapon of mass destruction, completely obliterating the studio set.

Ricky later explained why he was certain that John would cause maximum damage: 'When we were appearing together in the *Playing the Field* television series in 1998, John used to arrive on location in a swanky, sleek new sports car that was his pride and joy. He only had one way of driving, and that was with his foot glued to the accelerator.

'I used to arrive at the location in my old, clapped-out builder's van, because I was still doing some plastering work to help pay the bills. John gave me terrible stick over my coughing-and-spluttering van, and one day invited me to go for a drive with him in his sports car – "to see what a *real* drive is like". He wanted to impress me with how quickly the car could get away from a standing start. What he didn't take into account was the fact that he was parked on a cinders road. As he pushed his foot to the floor, the wheels spun and the car slid sideways right into the honey wagon. That is what we in the business call a mobile loo. An extra sitting doing his thing got the shock of his life as the wagon was shunted ten yards. He came out with his trousers around his ankles, stared madly at John and me and said, "Why the effing hell don't you find a conventional way of using the bog like everybody else!"'

So, later in this book – when you're reading about the celebrities behaving madly – remember that Ricky and many of his mates are up there with the best or worst of them.

I've known Ricky virtually all my life, and can vouch for the fact that he has hoarded hundreds of hilarious anecdotes about celebrities, plus their daftest quotes. I promise you'll have trouble putting his book down once you've picked it up. But that just might have something to do with the gum substance that the publishers have craftily worked into the cover.

Anyway, here's wishing you 'a lorra lorra' laughs with my alter ego, who is such a tight git that he's paying me with sheets of bog paper and trying to convince me they are old white fivers. He must think I'm as big an idiot as he is.

Ricky Tomlinson – a celebrity, my arse!

*Jim Royle*

# Curtain Up
## by Ricky Tomlinson

You may have read and laughed a lot at my *Football My Arse!* book. It sold like hot curry in Karachi, and the publishers were so pleased that they asked what other goodies I had in my collection of anecdotes.

It just so happens that throughout my life in the studio, on the screen – and in the prison cell – I have squirrelled away stories about celebrities like other people save pennies for a rainy day.

I have always been fascinated by celebrities, star struck even.

When I talk about celebrity, I don't mean those people who enjoy the fleeting fifteen minutes of fame that art guru Andy Warhol used to go on about.

I mean those who gather real stardust, the megastars who draw people to the cinema like moths to a flame, the champions of sport who thrill with their ability, the singers, musicians and stage performers who can hold an audience in the palm of their hands, the politicians and leaders with their motivational words that can move mountains.

I am talking REAL celebrities.

As my better half Jim Royle said in his deeply sincere introduction, celebrity comes too cheaply these days.

All you have to do is marry a footballer, make a fool of yourself on a reality television show, prove you can cook a sausage without burning it, hang wallpaper the right way up or grow a cauliflower and you can bask in the media spotlight. They will,

I promise, be getting plenty of stick in the following pages.

*Celebrities My Arse!*

Before summarising just what this book is about, I had better explain that prison cell reference for anybody who does not know that I was banged up for two years on what I considered to be a very dodgy conspiracy charge during my days as a building worker fighting for union justice.

One way I kept myself sane while in the nick was reading, reading, reading anything and everything I could get my mitts on. Biographies of celebrities were high on my list of reading material. I stored away in the cellar of my mind the funniest anecdotes, little knowing that one day I would be uncorking them and sharing them with you, dearest reader.

During my thirty-odd (very odd) years as an eager thespian I have been lucky enough to rub shoulders and often talk face to face with a procession of *real* celebrities.

I have worked extensively in television, and have made several films, filling in all the waiting time that comes with the job by swapping stories with my fellow actors. They have been the fount for much of my material, and I thank each and every one of them for their input to this book. They are too many to name, but they know who they are.

Another inspirational source has been my scriptwriting pal Norman Giller, who was a member of the *This Is Your Life* team for fourteen years, and got to hear scores of off-the-record stories. He also worked closely with comic genius Eric Morecambe, and included giants of comedy Benny Hill and Tommy Cooper among his associates. So I took Norm on board to help me trawl for celebrity-driven stories that, I hope, will amuse, entertain and sometimes enlighten you.

Many of the tales I'm about to tell are true, some are apocryphal, and in others I've changed the names to protect the guilty and also to save myself from legal fisticuffs. I don't wish to make any lawyer a celebrity.

Talking of lawyers, I loved the story that the late, lamented Leo

McKern told me about a run-in he had with a legal eagle while starring as Rumpole of the Bailey.

Leo was at his favourite bar at the Wig and Pen, the famous old pub opposite the Law Courts, when a lawyer who had supped a drink or three too many accosted him.

'You, sir,' said the eagle, 'would not sway any juror with your hammy delivery.'

'I beg to differ,' said Leo. 'I am convinced I could bring them to tears with my oratory. I bet you could not even begin to bring a tear to the eye.'

The lawyer took the bait. 'I could have you sobbing in your beer, sir,' insisted the lawyer.

'OK then, here's your chance to prove it,' said Leo. 'Bring a tear to *my* eye.'

With that he unscrewed his right eye and held it aloft. It was little known that our Horace Rumpole had a glass eye. Leo promised me that he ended the little contretemps by saying, 'Eye eye, that's yer lot!'

Welcome to *Celebrities My Arse!*

*Ricky Tomlinson*

# 1 Ho-ho-ho-Hollywood

Hooray for Hollywood. Where better to start my collection of off-beat stories about celebrities than in this Disneyland for grown-ups, where nothing is quite as it seems and where fame, fantasy and sheer farce are often on a collision course.

Celebrity in Hollywood is as necessary as breathing, and dictates an actor's bargaining power. The bigger the celebrity the more noughts on the cheque. Size does matter: it makes your fortune. That little bloke Tom Cruise has more noughts on his cheques than you'd find on an England cricket team's scorecard, yet off set he is famously lacking in inches.

Much to my embarrassment, I discovered somebody else who is very small and insignificant-looking when he's away from the silver screen. (A bit of name-dropping coming up here.) I was a guest of that master film director Roland Joffe (*The Killing Fields*, *The Mission*, etc.) at his fortieth birthday party back in the mid-eighties. It was held at the exclusive Groucho Club in Soho. I was the only bloke at the bash that I'd never heard of. A quick scan of the room took in *real* celebrities like Jeremy Irons, Liam Neeson, Ray McAnally, Cherie Lunghi, screenwriting genius Robert Bolt and distinguished producer David Lord Puttnam.

White-jacketed waiters hurried around with trayfuls of pink champagne, and there was enough food on the buffet table to feed an army. As I piled my plate, I found myself standing next to a small bloke. At last I'd found another unknown, like me! 'You in the business then?' I asked, trying to be friendly.

Just as he was about to answer a roar interrupted us. A giant birthday cake had popped open in the middle of the room, and a scantily dressed Marilyn Monroe lookalike clambered out and sang 'Happy Birthday' breathlessly to Roland, the man who had started me off down the acting road.

He made a witty speech of thanks, and then mingled with his guests. As Roland spotted me by the buffet he said: 'Ricky, glad you've met Bob.'

'Bob?' I said.

He pointed to the little man alongside me. 'Ricky Tomlinson, Robert De Niro,' he said by way of introduction.

I was gobsmacked. Robert De Niro, one of my heroes, who I had seen at least three times starring as Jake La Motta in my favourite boxing film *Raging Bull*.

The bloke I was being introduced to was small and weedy looking, with his hair pulled back in a ponytail and sporting a wispy goatee beard.

What an actor this man is! A chameleon who manages to look different in almost every film in which he appears.

So I got talking to my new pal Bobby De Niro, as you do. I told him how much I had loved his performance in *Raging Bull* and asked him about that memorable scene in which he asked his brother (played by Joe Pesci): 'Did you f*** my wife?'

I said that the shock on Pesci's face suggested he was hearing it for the first time, as if there had been no rehearsal.

'Sure we rehearsed it,' explained the master. 'But when it came to the actual take I asked, "Did you f*** your mother?" Joe had no idea that was coming and so was genuinely shocked. We dubbed in the "wife" line later.'

Long before I moved into such exalted company as Roland Joffe and Robert De Niro, I used to dream of being a Hollywood star when I was a kid growing up in Liverpool. The local cinemas – the Everton Picture Palace, the Hippodrome, the Majestic and the Lytton Cinema – became like a collective Tardis for me, taking me to places and adventures I could only dream about.

While most of the kids my age were into pretending they were cowboys like Roy Rogers, Hopalong Cassidy or Tom Mix, my imagination took in the real screen icons like Humphrey Bogart, Clark Gable, James Stewart, Jimmy Cagney and the smooth-as-silk Brits Cary Grant and David Niven.

I have been lucky enough to make quite a few films, but have never yet attracted the big Hollywood moguls. I can't understand why the phone is not ringing with offers to be leading man opposite the likes of Angelina Jolie and Jennifer Lopez. I'm sure Catherine Zeta-Jones would love the chance to snog me on set.

All right, hands up. I admit I haven't quite got the face to match the Brad Pitts and Johnny Depps of the film world. But I'd crawl across broken glass for the chance to star in just one Hollywood blockbuster so that I could act out my boyhood fantasies.

The nearest I got to appearing in a film with a Hollywood-type budget was when I played a villain in the action comedy *The 51st State*, with the larger-than-life Samuel L. Jackson as a kilt-wearing, golf-club-wielding, drug-making scientist. Don't know if they were trying to typecast me, but my role was that of a gay Scouse gangster suffering from haemorrhoids. It was a part I'd been itching to play.

There was I dreaming of Hollywood, and where was the location for the film? On my doorstep in Liverpool. It was shot at the peak of my popularity as Jim Royle, and the likeable Samuel Jackson looked on open mouthed as autograph hunters kept ambushing me and demanding that I write 'My arse' alongside my signature.

'What the hell is all that about?' Sam asked.

I explained about my role in *The Royle Family* and when I told him my catchphrase he rolled about laughing and said, 'Well kiss my black ass!'

This leads me nicely to kicking off my collection of Hollywood anecdotes with this one involving Samuel L. Jackson . . .

Samuel told me that when he was a kid, like me, he dreamed of being a Hollywood star, and he used to take his acting to extremes in the street games. One day he was playing soldiers with his pals, and decided to add a touch of reality. He took what he thought were bandages from his mother's bedroom, covered them with tomato ketchup and wrapped them around his head. Samuel went back into the street with all guns blazing, and was startled to find an elderly lady neighbour yelling at him that he was disgusting. 'Fancy wearing your mother's bloody sanitary towels around your head!' she said.

Robert Carlyle, one of Britain's finest all-round actors, is as Scottish as they come – a Glaswegian with a fierce and immense pride in his homeland. I have appeared in several films and television dramas with Robbie, and never cease to be amazed at his dedication and attention to detail. He invariably becomes the character he is playing. As that is often the psychopathic type, he can be odd company off the set.

Robbie was magnificent in *The 51st State*, playing a nutcase Liverpudlian villain with a Scouse accent as thick as a Mersey mist. I once had to phone him late at night at his hotel after he had gone to bed. My call woke him up, and he answered the telephone not in his natural Glaswegian brogue but in Scouse. Even asleep, he was in character!

Leonardo Di Caprio revealed how far we actors will go to mirror authenticity on the screen. I met him in a television studio during one of his publicity trips to the UK, and he talked about a scene he shot for the demanding director Martin Scorsese in *Gangs of New York*.

'I was doing a scene with Cameron Diaz,' he said, 'in which she had to slap my face over and over again. As we were preparing to shoot, Scorsese said: "Whenever Bob De Niro and I work together we always go for reality. If he were doing this scene with Cameron he would want to take real slaps."

'I thought if it was good enough for the great De Niro then it was good enough for me. About twenty takes later I was a bloody mess on the floor after taking more than forty full-blooded slaps. I looked up at Marty and said, "Are you happy with that, sir? Did we get it?"

'He patted me on the back and said, "You did great, kid. That was perfect. Now we need to shoot it from a few more angles . . ."'

I remember suffering similar punishment when I was shooting a scene as the potty football manager Mike Bassett. I had to fight the team mascot on the touchline, and bruised my hands punching his giant panda head. Scorsese and De Niro would have been proud of my dedication to the acting art!

Nobody throws themselves more into a part to try to get reality on the screen than Dustin Hoffman. When making *Marathon Man* with Laurence Olivier in 1976 he used to run for miles before shooting a scene so that he had the same breathless appearance as a marathon runner. Coming on set one day soaked with sweat and fighting for his breath, Olivier looked at him with some disdain and commented: 'Why don't you try acting, old boy?'

Hoffman's renowned quest for perfection and authenticity can, by all accounts, make him a pain in the arse to work with. He insisted on dressing as a woman off set while preparing for his role in *Tootsie* in 1982. When director Sidney Pollack was congratulated on an Oscar nomination for directing the film, he said: 'I'd give it up if I could have back the nine months of my life I spent with Dustin making it.'

For years Hollywood agents and publicists fought to hide the fact that Rock Hudson was as bent as a nine-pound note. There were veiled hints to any journalists nosing around with thoughts of breaking the story that they would, so to speak, have their arses sued.

So imagine the scene at a press conference in Hollywood to launch one of Hudson's films with Doris Day when a young journalist cleared her throat and said hesitantly, 'Mr Hudson, I would like to ask you about the persistent rumour . . .'

[Picture here publicists, producers and agents breaking out in bubbles of perspiration . . .']

'. . . that you have had your teeth capped.'

Sharon Stone got her knickers in a twist over her famous leg-cross performance in *Basic Instinct*. Well, that's not quite true because she wasn't wearing any. She later revealed – and revealed is the operative word – that director Paul Verhoeven had tricked her into filming the scene knickerless. After a couple of takes, the director instructed her to remove her underwear because it was visible through her dress. 'I shot the scene,' Sharon said, 'and then found out that it had not been necessary. When I realised what had happened I slapped Paul's face.'

I guess it was a bit of a naughty trick, but it produced a classic scene that burned itself into the minds of every red-blooded male who saw it.

When I appeared on a Michael Parkinson show, I was delighted to find that one of the other guests was megastar Sir Sean Connery. We had a long chat in the green room and it was good to discover that he had none of the 'big-I-am' attitude that clings to too many people who make it into the major-star category.

I was amazed when Sean told me that he had virtually no formal education, and that he had left school at thirteen during the Second World War. It made my five years at Venice Street secondary school in Liverpool seem, in contrast, like high academia. Like me, Sean picked up just about everything he knows in the university of life and I really felt like he was a kindred spirit.

It's astonishing what he has achieved as an actor considering his start in life, and he deserves every ounce of his celebrity.

I told him my honest opinion that he was the best Bond by miles, and his eyes sort of clouded. 'I hate that bloody James Bond,' he said. 'I'd like to kill him. But I guess I'm stuck with him until I go to my box.'

It has been a quarter of a century since he last played the part, and still idiots like me are reminding him that Bond is the character we associate him with, despite a procession of wonderful screen performances post-007.

Sean made his debut as Bond in the *Dr No* classic of 1962. When released in Japan they changed the title to *We Don't Want a Doctor*! They managed to make it sound like a *Carry On* film.

Just before going on set for his interview with Parky, Sean made an undisguised check of his flies. 'I once sat through an entire chat show with my fly undone,' he said. 'It was the most revealing interview I've ever given.'

Wesley Snipes listened respectfully when Sean Connery took him to one side during the shooting of the 1993 film *Rising Sun* and gave him some unique acting advice. 'When you're doing scenes in a car – whether it's the front or back seat – do it with your trousers off,' said Sean. 'The car is always baking because of the camera lights, but the audience only see your top half. You will be much cooler and give a better performance if you're wearing just boxers.'

Snipes said later: 'I've never been able to watch Sean on the screen since without remembering that advice and wondering what he's wearing – or, rather, not wearing – down below out of shot.'

One of the most underrated films in Sean Connery's extraordinary output is *The Man Who Would Be King*, in which he co-starred with Michael Caine. It was an inspired pairing of two British actors by director John Huston, who said: 'I did not have to give

Michael Parkinson (centre) invited the actor considered the world's sexiest man on to his chat show. There I am on his left, with Canadian big band singer Michael Bublé alongside me. Also on the show was that muppet of an MP Boris Johnson (second left). Oh yes, and Sean Connery (left) topped the bill. He did not take kindly to me telling him he was the best of the Bonds. 'I hate that bloody James Bond,' he said. 'I'd like to kill him.' Sounds like a job for 007.

Sean and Michael any direction apart from say "Action". They were perfectly cast. The only direction I gave Michael was that he could talk a little quicker. It worked.'

I have been an avid Caine watcher right from his early days in *Zulu*, the Harry Palmer films and *Alfie*. His approach to celebrity should be a blueprint for anybody who makes it to superstardom. 'If I am approached in the street I try to be polite and appreciative that somebody is taking their time to acknowledge me,' he said. 'I will not be speeding by in a limousine with two blondes and a bottle of champagne. Mind you, I suppose that does have its appeal!'

There was a time when Sir Michael might have been that one with the champers. I listened to him once reminiscing on his wild days, of which his memories are hazy.

The interviewer asked him if there was a particular wild week-end that he could remember.

'There was a wildest weekend that I *don't* remember,' Caine replied. 'One Saturday evening during a London run of *The Long, The Short and The Tall* I went on the town with Peter O'Toole. Big mistake!

'Some time later we woke up side by side on a bed in some strange place. We were fully clothed. A woman neither of us could recognise came into the room, and said, "Hello boys." I asked where we were, and she said Hampstead. We did not have a clue how we had got there.

'Peter looked at his watch, squinting through his hangover. "Is it morning or night?" he asked.

'"It's morning," she said.

'"God," said Peter. "Sunday morning already. Whatever happened to Saturday night."

'"No," said the woman. "It's *Monday* morning."

'All we found out about what happened that weekend is that we had both been banned for life from a fast food restaurant in Leicester Square. For doing what and to whom I have no idea.

'And we never did find out whose house we were in, how we got there or the name of the lady.'

'Was she attractive?' asked the interviewer.

'Uh, not attractive enough to find out who she was,' came the reply.

Having played Bobby Grant for years in *Brookside*, I feel that I'm keeping it in the family when I say that the name Grant has been synonymous with Hollywood for a stretch of more than seventy years.

First of all, of course, came Cary Grant, who started life in Bristol as Archibald Leach. He was the world's most admired and imitated sophisticated man across four decades, and brought a touch of class to every part that he played. In 1986, the very year that he passed on to the great studio in the sky, along came Hugh Grant making his movie debut.

Like Cary before him, Hugh has made a career out of being an intelligent comic leading man with that edge of English eccentricity that is a magnet at the box office.

Cary had a sharp sense of humour off as well as on the screen. When a reporter wired his agent to ask, 'How old Cary Grant?' Cary himself picked up the message and replied, 'Old Cary Grant well. How you?'

Four-times-married Cary managed to keep a low profile with his private life despite living in the magnified goldfish bowl that is Hollywood. He was once hit with a paternity suit (later dropped) on the eve of collecting an honorary Oscar at the age of sixty-six, and in contrast was for a long time the centre of rumours about his very close association with fellow star Randolph Scott that included twelve years of sharing the same house.

The one thing that Cary did admit to was taking more than one hundred LSD trips in the 1960s. He described the drug-taking as medical experiments to try to come to terms with a troubled childhood during which his mother was placed in a mental home when he was just nine.

'Everybody', he said, 'would like to be Cary Grant – including me.' He never quite managed to escape his past as Archie Leach.

His namesake Hugh Grant, and successor to the throne of Hollywood's favourite suave, debonair Englishman, seemed to have 'blown' his career almost before it had started when he got involved in the headline-hitting sex scandal with Sunset Strip prostitute Divine Brown in 1995.

He was arrested by LA police after being caught in a parked car while Divine was showing that the vehicle had good head room. Hugh had paid her a reported $50 for her services, and ended up paying a $1,500 fine and getting splashed all over the front pages. Blown out of all proportion, you might say.

Hugh managed to turn the bad publicity on its head with a superbly organised PR campaign. Appearing on the hugely popular Jay Leno television chat show within a week of the Brown episode, he responded to the question 'What the hell were you thinking?' with 'I'm not one to go round blowing my own trumpet . . .'

The rest of the reply was lost in gales of laughter from the audience, and his career was back up and running. Blow me, his video sales shot up by more than a third the week after his TV confession.

Another of the Grant dynasty – Richard E. – is famously teetotal. In his first starring role in *Withnail & I* he had several scenes in which he had to get violently drunk. Writer/director Bruce Robinson persuaded him to get paralytic so that he could experience what it was like. 'I felt awful for days afterwards,' said Richard, 'and I now consider myself fortunate to be allergic to alcohol. My father, a wonderfully charming and amusing man when sober, was a violent alcoholic and that is a schizophrenia that I would rather do without.'

I often see the marvellously smooth actor David Niven described as the quintessential Englishman. There's just the little matter that he was Scottish. He summed up the mad, mad, mad world of the acting profession beautifully: 'We get wonderfully overpaid for dressing up and playing games. By any stretch of the imagination, it can hardly be called work.'

Speaking as somebody who spent twenty years sweating buckets as a plasterer, I can second that opinion.

The famous David Niven story that he told on just about every chat show that had a bleeping machine went like this: 'Bogart and I used to take the mickey out of Billy Wilder's heavy Austrian accent. Billy had an acerbic manner, and when once overhearing Bogie and I mimicking him he said: "You clever dicks think I know f*** nothing. Well let me tell you I know f*** all!"'

Wilder had one of the most creative brains in Hollywood, as well as one of the shrewdest. Ignoring the sarcastic remarks of friends, he started building a collection of way-out modern art in the 1930s. Forty years later it was valued at more than $40 million.

He had a fantastic idea for an opening shot of a film he was planning for the comeback of Laurel and Hardy. The picture would open with a panning shot of the famous HOLLYWOOD sign, and then the camera would zoom in to show Stan and Ollie sleeping together in one of the Os. Sadly Ollie became ill, the film was never made and the shot remained in Wilder's wonderful imagination.

Sir Anthony Hopkins – still proudly Welsh but now an American citizen – was invited to have dinner at the White House with President Bill Clinton and First Lady Hillary, shortly after the release of *Hannibal*, the sequel to *The Silence of the Lambs* (in which Hopkins starred as Hannibal 'the Cannibal' Lecter). 'I presume', said Sir Anthony on receiving the invitation, 'that we will be having a finger buffet?'

When he was paired with Emma Thompson in *Howards End*, he received a note from Emma's mother that read: 'Please don't eat her!'

Sir Anthony is one of the most versatile actors of all time. He has played many real-life people on the screen, including such diverse personalities as William Bligh, David Lloyd George, Richard the Lionheart, Pablo Picasso, Yitzhak Rabin, Adolf Hitler and American Presidents John Quincy Adams and Richard Nixon . . . and he does an uncannily accurate impersonation of the comedian Tommy Cooper. Just like that . . .

He is also an accomplished pianist and painter, yet because of severe dyslexia was considered a dummy at school. One part he played too well was that of an alcoholic and at one stage he thought he was going mad before he kicked the habit. 'I got hooked on tequila and believed I was John the Baptist,' he recalled. 'I used to talk to the sea and, funny thing, the sea talked back to me. It was weird.'

I love Sir Anthony's approach to whether to accept or turn down a role. 'First of all I read the script,' he said. 'If I am happy with that I consider the location. If it's a nice place to be then I look at all the noughts in the offer being made.

Sir Anthony Hopkins, who found Jodie Foster so appetising when he was giving his Oscar-winning performance as Hannibal Lecter in *The Silence of the Lambs*. Well, she does look good enough to eat.

'Then I invariably say "yes" because it's better than working for a living. I don't give a damn whether it's a good career move and all that bull.'

My kind of man. And what a bloody great actor.

Burt Reynolds and Clint Eastwood were young actors together in the 1950s, and both got fired by Universal. Reynolds recalled: 'Clint got the boot because his Adam's apple stuck out too far, he had a chipped tooth and he talked too slow. When I asked why they were firing me they said, "You can't act." I said to Clint, "You're really screwed, man. I can learn to act, but you can't get rid of that Adam's apple." It really held his career back, didn't it!'

Meryl Streep, one of the finest actresses of our time, had a harrowing scene to shoot in *Sophie's Choice* and took a long time mentally preparing herself for the performance. The storyline was that she had to stand in line in a Nazi concentration camp and, with a bullying German guard threatening her, select one of her two children to be sent for extermination.

Publicising her autobiography, Meryl called it the most emotionally draining scene of her career.

She gave what she knew was her best effort, and as the child was snatched from her grasp waited for distinguished director Alan J. Pakula to shout 'Cut!'

There was an unusually long delay, and Meryl thought, 'My God, he's overwhelmed by it . . .'

She stole a glance towards the veteran director and found him with his head back, fast asleep!

The late, great Sir John Mills, who became a close personal friend of mine in his later years, told me a wonderful story about how he was once shopping in Oxford Street at the peak of his fame. He saw a shirt he quite fancied in a shop window and went in to see if they had one in his size.

'My goodness,' preened the manager. 'Sir John Mills in *my* shop. Please let me have your autograph.'

While Sir John was signing, the manager telephoned his wife. 'You'll never guess who I've got in my shop,' he said.

He handed the telephone to Sir John and asked him to say 'hello' to his wife.

Flattered by all the attention, Sir John bought six shirts and a couple of ties.

'Will you take a cheque?' he asked.

'Of course,' said the manager, 'provided you have some sort of identification.'

A similar thing happened in recent times to Sir Ian McKellen, when appearing at the London premiere of *Lord of the Rings*.

'As I got out of the chauffeur-driven Rolls-Royce alongside the red carpet in Leicester Square,' he recalled, 'there was an enormous roar. It was the sort of welcome I thought was reserved for the likes of The Beatles or The Rolling Stones.

'There were more than fifteen thousand people jammed into the Square, and I did my best to meet as many as I possibly could. Finally I pulled myself away from the clamouring autograph-hunters and made my way to the entrance.

'A uniformed job's-worth barred my way, and said: "Excuse me, have you got a ticket?"

'I forgot that I had a ticket tucked away in my pocket, and said: "No, afraid not."

'"In that case," said Job's-worth, "you can't come in."

'"But I'm in the movie," I said, "and I'm due on stage with the director any moment now."

'"That's what they all say, sir," said Job's-worth.

'"You have no idea who I am, do you?" I said, feeling a little irritated but also embarrassed for the man who could not win this one.

'I turned back to face the crowd and waved. Fifteen thousand people waved back and roared.

'"Well they seem to know me," I said.

'"OK," said Job's-worth. "You've made your point. In you go . . ."'

One of my all-time favourite Hollywood tales is almost certainly apocryphal, but that doesn't make it any less funny. In the biblical epic *The Greatest Story Ever Told*, John 'Duke' Wayne appeared as a Roman centurion who leads Jesus to the cross on which he is to be crucified.

Wayne had only one line to deliver: 'Truly, this was the Son of God.'

Director George Stevens allowed him three takes before having a quiet word with him. 'Duke,' he said, 'you're talking about the Son of God here. You've got to deliver the line with a little more awe.'

Wayne nodded his understanding and returned to his mark, ready to give it his best shot.

He looked up at the cross and declared: '*Aaaaww*, truly this was the Son of God.'

An equally famous Hollywood story handed down through generations revolves around the legendary director Cecil B. De Mille. He called a production meeting on the morning of the making of the key scene for one of his heavily populated biblical epics.

It involved a bridge collapsing, thousands of gallons of water gushing through the set in a realistic-looking tidal wave and hundreds of gladiators being swept away.

'We get only one shot at this,' De Mille said to his crew. 'Give it your total concentration and let's get it in the can without mishap.'

They rehearsed throughout the morning, and then De Mille decided to go for the one take immediately after lunch.

'Action!' he shouted, and right on cue the bridge collapsed, the water gushed, the gladiators fell into the waves and huge pillared buildings toppled. It had all gone as planned.

'Did you get that, Camera One?' shouted De Mille through his megaphone.

'Just perfect,' came the response.

'Camera Two?'

'Everything went swimmingly.'

'Camera Three?'

'Couldn't have been better.'

De Mille then pointed his megaphone to the top of the hill that had been built on the far side of the studio from where he could get the best panoramic view of the bridge collapsing.

'How about you, Camera Four?' he shouted.

'Ready when you are, Mr De Mille . . .'

I have always been fascinated by the life and times of the madly eccentric and massively talented Howard Hughes, who was renowned for his sexual appetite in his days as a big-shot producer before he became a potty recluse. It was a favourite boast of his that he had deflowered two hundred virgins while working in Hollywood.

'That', said acid-tongued Las Vegas comedian Jimmy the Greek, 'means he had every one of them.'

Among his known conquests were some of the most glamorous actresses of his time: Bette Davis, Katharine Hepburn, Jane Russell, Olivia De Havilland and Ava Gardner. Bette Davis wrote in one of her memoirs that when he made love to her he used to close his eyes and pretend she was a man! Now that's what you call acting.

Hughes, of course, became seriously rich. He owned the Las Vegas television station KLAS (Channel 8), and he insisted they show films throughout the night to help him get through his insomnia. If he fell asleep and missed a key scene, he would phone up in the middle of the night and instruct them to rewind the film to where he had nodded off.

He was convinced people were stealing his ideas, and so when he used to speak in public he would keep a hand over his mouth so that nobody could lip-read.

In his peak years as the most infamous stud in Hollywood he stood six-foot-four and weighed in at a muscular fifteen stone. After his final years as an unhinged recluse he was found dead with six-inch-long toenails, matted hair down to his shoulders and weighing just over six stones.

Final word to the unique man: 'Me a paranoid, deranged multimillionaire? God damn it, get your facts right. I'm a billionaire.'

Clark Gable was the undisputed King of Hollywood when I first became captured by the world of movies. He was a huge box-office draw despite having ears that would not have looked out of place on a baby elephant.

Howard Hughes, a master of the one-line put-down, said: 'They made him look like a taxicab with both doors open.'

Comedian Milton Berle called them 'the best ears of our lives'.

Yet he was one of the biggest male sex symbol stars of all time. When he revealed to Claudette Colbert in *It Happened One Night* that he never wore a vest, the underwear industry reeled from falling sales.

Gable tried to shrug off his reputation for the ladies. 'Hell,' he said, 'if I'd jumped all the dames I'm supposed to have jumped I'd have no time to go fishing.'

According to his then wife Carole Lombard he 'was never like the Clark Gable of the movies in bed'!

She once gave him a hand-knitted willie warmer as a Christmas present, writing acidly: 'It did not take very long to knit it. If he had one inch less he would not be the King of Hollywood, he would be the queen!'

With wives like that, who needs enemies?

Frankly, my dear, he did not give a damn.

Humphrey Bogart was right up there with Clark Gable as a hero in my cinema escapism days. Nobody has got near him for being able to play cynical yet amiable tough guys, and he made the trench coat and trilby combination the coolest thing in fashion.

Bogie never took himself too seriously, unlike some of the current so-called stars. He once said: 'I have made more lousy pictures than any other actor in history.'

That sort of brutal honesty would not sit well in today's Hollywood, where everybody goes to work on a huge ego.

From all accounts he was good company until he'd had a drink or three too many. It was famous Hollywood restaurateur Dave Chasen who summed him up: 'Bogart's a helluva nice guy until about eleven o'clock when he suddenly starts to think he's Bogart.'

Asked if he would change anything if he could have his life over again, Bogie said: 'Yeah, I'd stick to Scotch and not switch to martinis.'

Gable and Bogie were at the peak of their popularity when hire-and-fire-'em producers like Harry Cohn and Sam Goldwyn ruled the Hollywood roost.

I cannot let this Hollywood collection go without dipping into their power-mad world.

The tyrannical Cohn was the little-loved and largely loathed boss of Columbia Pictures for more than thirty years from 1924. When he died in 1958, comedy actor Red Skelton said as huge crowds turned out for Cohn's funeral: 'It proves what Harry always said – give the public what they want to see and they'll come out to see it.'

Another Hollywood veteran with scars to show for his run-ins with Cohn reportedly said at the funeral: 'They're all here for the same reason as me . . . to make sure he's dead.'

Hedda Hopper, actress turned vitriolic columnist, commented: 'You had to stand in line to hate Harry Cohn.'

Frank Sinatra weighed in with: 'He had a sense of humour like an open grave.'

It was Cohn himself who once said: 'I don't get ulcers . . . I give them.'

With his East European background, school drop-out Cohn was continually mangling the English language yet still insisted on reading every script and making changes wherever he felt necessary.

Screenwriter Clifford Odets recalled: 'We were once having a script meeting about a biblical film when Harry stormed into the office. "God damn it!" he roared. "Do I have to do everything around here? Which of you college goons wrote this?"

'"Wrote what?" we chorused.

'"These 'yes, sirees' and 'no, sirees' lines. I may not have been college-educated but I sure as hell know they didn't go around saying that in biblical times."

'I took the script from him and read the offending lines aloud, "Yes, sire" . . . "no, sire."'

Another time Cohn threw a script on to the desk and screamed at his writers: 'The speeches in here are crap. Total crap. Why can't you give me classy stuff that the audience will recognise immediately?'

'You mean like Hamlet's soliloquy?'

'God damn it, no!' shouted Cohn. 'I don't mean that Hamlet feller. Give me some stuff from Shakespeare . . . that "To be or not to be" business.'

Sam Goldwyn, the archetypal movie mogul, did even stranger things with the English language than Cohn. Here are just a handful of the classics attributed to him that have gone down in film folklore:

'A verbal agreement isn't worth the paper it's written on.'

'In two words – im-possible.'

'Tell me, how did you love the picture?'

'Our comedies are not to be laughed at.'

'Why the hell don't our screen writers come up with some new clichés?'

'Anybody who goes to a psychiatrist should have his head examined.'

'I had a great idea this morning, but I didn't like it.'

'Gentlemen, kindly include me out.'

'Our latest film is more than magnificent. It's mediocre.'

'You have to take the bull between your teeth.'

'I'll give you a definite maybe.'

'What we want is a story that starts with an earthquake and works its way up to a climax.'

'Directors are always biting the hand that lays the golden eggs.'

'We have all passed a lot of water since then.'

'Let's bring it up to date with some snappy nineteenth-century dialogue.'

Humphrey Bogart was a real man's man, yet like so many Hollywood 'giants' he was short in stature. Did you know that in his greatest film role, as Rick Blaine in *Casablanca*, he had to wear platforms on his shoes so that he could look Ingrid Bergman in the eye when saying his great line: 'Here's lookin' at you, kid'?

Other short-arses who walk tall on the silver screen include Tom Cruise, Steve McQueen, Fred Astaire, Gene Kelly, Edward G. Robinson, Al Pacino, Dustin Hoffman, Richard Dreyfuss, Woody Allen, Spencer Tracy, James Cagney, Jack Nicholson, George Raft and, of course, the mighty shrimp Alan Ladd, who used to have to stand on a box to kiss his leading ladies.

Little is as it appears in Hollywood. There are enough hair-pieces on virtually every set to keep a flock of shorn sheep warm. Bogie wore a wig, as did Bing Crosby, Frank Sinatra, Fred Astaire, Gary Cooper, Henry Fonda, Sean Connery, George Burns, David Niven, James Stewart, Charlton Heston, Charles Boyer, Gene Kelly, Tony Curtis, Peter Sellers and modern follicly challenged stars like Ted Danson, Samuel L. Jackson, Bruce Willis, William Shatner and Burt Reynolds.

When it was first revealed that George Burns wore a rug he went berserk and threatened to punch the writer who had outed him.

'But I didn't think you'd mind,' said the scribe.

'If I didn't mind,' shot back George, 'why the hell would I wear a toupee?'

Face lifts and breast implants are so common in Hollywood that almost the only people wearing unaided smiles are the surgeons.

The most common op is the nose job, and among those who have faced the camera with revamped conks are Dean Martin, Marilyn Monroe, Peter O'Toole, George Hamilton, Dinah Shore, Joel Grey, Raquel Welch, Stefanie Powers, Rita Moreno, Pamela Anderson, Dolly Parton, *Friends* stars Lisa Kudrow and Jennifer Aniston, and Cher, who is a walking monument to the wonders of cosmetic surgery. As for Michael Jackson, he's had so much refurbishment work that I hear he's got his own mafia of surgeons – the cosa nostril.

I can deny those rumours that I have had a nose job. My schnoz is my trademark, and the make-up girls had great fun building it into a W. C. Fields style of bulbous delight when I was playing the part of Jim Royle.

Can you imagine Jim going in for some rhinoplasty? Nose job, my arse!

# You've gotta laugh

A leading actor in many B-movies walks into a Hollywood bar and orders a triple Scotch. The barman gives it to him and he gulps it down with one tilt of his head.

'Hey buddy, you must be having it rough,' says the bartender. 'What's the problem?'

'Well, I got home early from the studio last night and found my wife and my co-star in bed with each other!'

'That's terrible, pal,' says the sympathetic bartender. 'Have this one on the house.'

The bartender gives him another triple Scotch, and again he throws it down in one go.

'If you don't mind me asking,' says the bartender, 'what did you say to your wife?'

'What could I say?' says the actor. 'I've told her that it's all over. After this there can only be divorce.'

'You're right, buddy,' says the bartender. 'To do that behind your back is unforgivable. So what did you say to your co-star?'

The actor downed another triple Scotch before he could bring himself to answer.

'Well, I knocked him off the bed,' he says, 'and shouted, "You're a bad dog, Lassie."'

# Hark who's talking about the film world

**Sir Anthony Hopkins:**
'I have a punishing workout regimen. Every day I do three minutes on the treadmill, then I lie down, drink a glass of vodka and smoke a cigarette.'

**Tony Curtis:**
*(asked what it was like to kiss Marilyn Monroe in* Some Like It Hot*)*
'It was like kissing Hitler.'

**James Cagney:**
'One thing that troubles me is that they say that my portrayals of gangsters and hoodlums led to a tolerance of the criminal element by society. Well, I certainly hope they didn't, because I'm firmly opposed to crime.'

**Tom Cruise:**
'The exciting part of acting are those moments when you surprise yourself.'

**Al Pacino:**
'My first language as a kid was shy. It's only by having been thrust into the limelight that I have learned to cope with my shyness.'

**Paul Newman:**
'To work as hard as I have to achieve something worthwhile in the movie world and then have some yo-yo come up and say, "Take off those dark glasses and let's see those blue eyes" is totally discouraging.'

**Johnny Depp:**
'I don't pretend to be Captain Weird. I just do what I do.'

**John Travolta:**
'I'm not an old-fashioned romantic. I believe in love and marriage, but not necessarily with the same person.'

**Bob Hope:**
'You can calculate Zsa Zsa Gabor's age by the rings on her fingers.'

**Don Rickles:**
'Just look at poor Ernest Borgnine. I wonder if anyone else was hurt in the accident?'

**Carrie Fisher:**
'You can't find true affection in Hollywood because everyone does the fake affection so well.'

**Lauren Bacall:**
'Hollywood is the only place where an amicable divorce means that each gets fifty per cent.'

**Errol Flynn:**
'They've great respect for the dead in Hollywood, but none for the living.'

**Sir Alec Guinness:**
'An actor is at his best a kind of unfrocked priest who, for an hour or two, can call on heaven and hell to mesmerise a group of innocents.'

**Sir Ralph Richardson:**
'Acting is merely the art of keeping a large group of people from coughing.'

**Sir John Gielgud:**
'Ah, dear Ingrid Bergman – speaks five languages and can't act in any of them.'

**Sir John Mills:**
'I have worked with more submarines than leading ladies.'

**Spencer Tracy:**
*(on the secrets of acting)*
'Know your lines, and don't bump into the furniture.'

**Alfred Hitchcock:**
'If I made *Cinderella* they'd be looking for a body in the coach.'

**Mae West:**
'A hard man is good to find.'

**Shirley Temple:**
'I stopped believing in Santa Claus at the age of six. My mother took me to see him in a department store and he asked me for my autograph.'

**Clark Gable:**
'I'm no actor. Never have been. What the people see up there on that screen is me.'

**Cher:**
'I think the longer I look good, the better gay men feel.'

**Charles Bronson:**
'I look like a quarry someone has dynamited, but I ain't complaining.'

**Arnold Schwarzenegger:**
'The worst thing I can be is the same as everybody else. I hate that.'

**Cecil B. De Mille:**
*(arguing with the studio over the escalating costs of* The Ten Commandments*)*
'So what d'you want me to do? Stop shooting now and release it as *The Five Commandments*?'

**Roger Moore:**
'My acting range? Left eyebrow raised, right eyebrow raised.'

**Ava Gardner:**
'I do everything for a reason. Most of the time the reason is money.'

**Lew Grade:**
*(regretting ever getting involved in the disaster movie* Raise the Titanic*)*
'It would have been cheaper to lower the Atlantic.'

**Humphrey Bogart:**
'You're not a star until they can spell your name in Karachi.'

**Orson Welles:**
'A movie studio is the best toy a boy ever had.'

# 2 **Unreal Celebrities**

From the sublime to the bloody ridiculous . . . from Hollywood to Cricklewood – from *real* celebrities of the cinema to people who have become famous just for being famous. From legends of the screen to nobodies who are barely legends in their own lunchtime. Yet, thanks to the new phenomenon of reality television, they wear the cloak of celebrity.

Reality television is the curse of the modern actor. I have many talented actor friends who can't get any vital TV exposure because our screens are stuffed with wall-to-wall reality shows such as *Big Brother*, *I'm a Celebrity, Get Me Out of Here!* and a dozen cheap and cheerless clones.

It is all filling TV time that used to be allotted to entertaining variety shows, well-scripted drama, sitcoms and classic serials. Good actors and versatile entertainers have been knocked off the screen to make way for nonentities very briefly becoming famous by talking nonsense on national television for boring hours on end. Celebrities, my arse!

Struggling along with the actors to get TV work are an army of producers, directors, writers and production staff, whose collective talent is not needed in the making of programmes that seem to me to be aimed at the brain-dead.

I have often been asked to appear on celebrity reality shows.

My stock answer is: 'I'd rather take the dog for a walk, thank you.' Or much stronger words to that effect.

It makes me wonder how desperate people have become that they will agree to take part in genital-eating trials in the jungle, or expose themselves to ridicule by spending time with total strangers with whom they would not normally want to be seen dead.

George Galloway, for example, surrendered every ounce of what integrity he had left when he agreed to go into the open prison that is the *Big Brother* house.

From being a Member of Parliament for his Respect party, he instantly became a member of the funny club and completely *dis*respected.

He suddenly found himself trying to make conversation with a cross-dresser, a sex-mad basketball player covered in tattoos, a manic-depressive Page 3 model, a rapper called Maggot, Sven-Göran Eriksson's ex-bit-on-the-side, an emaciated Michael Barrymore, an out-of-work actress, and a non-celebrity who had to pretend she was a celebrity (and paradoxically came out of it the biggest celebrity of them all!).

Welcome to television in the twenty-first century. 'Gorgeous George' had not been surrounded by so many screwball people since, well, his last appearance in Parliament.

There have been few more toe-curling, humiliating scenes on television than the sight of Galloway on all fours in front of Rula Lenska purring and pretending to be a cat. It screamed out for George to be doctored.

If this can be described as good television then I'm a Dutchman's uncle ('Velcome aboard, Ricky van Tomlinson').

I have deliberately used a Dutch metaphor because *Big Brother*, the first of the major modern reality shows, was born and bred in Holland. A pity it didn't stay there.

It was the brainchild of John de Mol, and developed by his production company Endemol. It has featured as a prime-time programme in more than seventy countries and has made them a damfull of money while dumbing down television to numbing depths.

Here's Craig Phillips all done up like a dog's dinner when collecting an award on behalf of *Big Brother* for the best reality show on television. Craig donated his prize money to help pay for a close pal to have a life-saving operation. He's a Scouser with real heart and we're very proud of him in Liverpool.

My fellow Liverpudlian Craig Phillips was the first winner of the British version of *Big Brother*, and he is one product of reality television who I believe deserves his celebrity. He gave his prize money to a friend for a life-saving operation. What a classy guy. I have got to know Craig well since he came into our lives through the show, and we have a respect for each other because of the trades in which we served our time. He is a master carpenter and I have certificates (and thousands of walls and ceilings) to prove that I am a skilled plasterer. Craig and I have got together to show television viewers how to do up old houses properly, not the slap-dash stuff you see on too many do-it-yourself programmes. When I watch some of the so-called DIY experts giving advice I fully expect the house they're working in to fall down.

Caroline Aherne and Craig Cash cleverly created a sort of reality television with their comedy classic *The Royle Family*, in which I was lucky to have the role of lazy slob Jim Royle (some described it as typecasting).

But unlike the inane talk of much of the reality programmes this was all beautifully scripted for a cast of marvellous actors, so well scripted in fact that Jim won me the Comedy Actor of the Year award. Ta very much.

From what I have seen of 'real' reality television, it features people running off at the mouth without a scriptwriter's necessary punctuation marks and hand signals. They continually make fools of themselves at the altar of the great god of television. I can think of better things to do with my precious time on this planet.

Our must-watch programmes on the box used to include *The Morecambe and Wise Show* and *Sunday Night at the London Palladium*, with Tommy Trinder, Bruce Forsyth and Jimmy Tarbuck introducing megastars such as Sammy Davis Jr, Norman Wisdom, Tommy Cooper and Nat King Cole.

Now topping the menu is *I'm a Celebrity, Get Me Out of Here!* Don't try to tell me that C-list celebrities wrestling with rats in the jungle is better entertainment than Ken Dodd, Mario Lanza or The Beatles topping the *Sunday Night at the London Palladium* bill (as they did among a procession of other major stars).

Where's the dignity and decency gone when Carol Thatcher – daughter of our former Prime Minister – can win the *I'm a Celebrity* series after eating the testicles of a kangaroo live on television?

But at least the TV companies have retained some taste. They refused to show repeats of Ms Thatcher crouching and relieving herself alongside her hammock.

I can almost hear dear old Eric Morecambe saying: 'Phew, that's a relief. What d'you think of it so far?'

*Rubbish!* Or, as Ms Thatcher might say, 'Wubbish!'

So who's to blame for reality television? The finger of suspicion – or should that be derision? – points at Allen Funt, a bald-as-a-coot American with a college education and a love of nonsense humour. He was the ideas man who, back in 1947, came up with a new radio programme for American audiences called *Candid Microphone*. A year later it reappeared as *Candid Camera*, the world's first regular reality TV show. It aired every Sunday night on coast-to-coast ABC television, and quickly gained a huge audience of voyeuristic lovers of the absurd.

It gradually caught on across the globe, and 'Smile, you're on *Candid Camera*' became an international catchphrase. Presenters of the UK version included Bob Monkhouse and Jonathan Routh. Among the classic scams were free-wheeling a motorcar with no engine downhill into a garage, and asking the mechanic to take a look under the bonnet to see why the car was not running properly, plus accelerating a conveyor belt to treble speed as workers tried to put in cake fillings.

Another featured Peter Dulay pretending to eat a goldfish from a bowl on a shop counter (it was actually a slice of carrot). It backfired when a mother complained that her son had watched the programme, and had emulated Dulay by swallowing the family pet.

'My idea for *Candid Camera* was to have people acting naturally without rehearsal or script,' explained Funt. 'When people know a camera is watching them they become unnatural and either withdrawn or exhibitionist.'

Little did he know that his idea of reality television would grow into the monster it is today. The difference from the *Candid Camera* concept is that nowadays the participants *do* know they are being watched by the all-seeing camera and heard by the latest in digital microphones. They react in most cases by making prats of themselves.

One reality television programme that even I find acceptable is *The Apprentice*, the brainchild of British-born Mark Burnett. It became the number-one show on American television, with

Donald Trump in the hiring and firing chair. Sir Alan Sugar has proved himself a TV natural in the British version.

Mind you, just for a laugh, I'd love to sit facing the acid-tongued Sir Alan as one of his hopeful apprentices and say to his face: 'Oi, mate, I wouldn't want to work for you as long as you've got a hole in your arse.'

Purely for the purposes of putting together this book, I have forced myself to look deeper into the phenomenon of instant celebrity through the medium of reality television shows. Now I wish to share the cringiest moments with you in the hope that you will join my one-man campaign to bring properly scripted, quality programmes back to our screens.

The queen of the reality show celebrities has surely got to be Jade Goody, whose IQ seems smaller than her shoe size. I have collected these Goody goodies from her performance in the *Big Brother* house . . .

When a fellow housemate said he lived in Cambridge, she responded: 'I'm from Bermondsey and I know that's London, but where's Cambridge?'

He told her it was in East Anglia. Jade replied: 'Where's East Angular [*sic*] though? I thought that was abroad.'

It got better. 'I knew Lynne was from Aberdeen,' she said later. 'But I didn't realise Aberdeen was in Scotland.'

More matters geographical: 'Rio de Janeiro, ain't that a person?'

Moving closer to home: 'Do they speak Portuganese in Portugal? I thought Portugal was in Spain.'

Her knowledge of the Midlands was no better: 'Have they got seasides in Birmingham?'

Jade on the national flag: 'The Union Jack is for all of us, but the St George is just for London, ain't it?'

When it was suggested Jade might be best off moving to the United States, she responded: 'They do speak English, don't they?'

She was not too strong on the Middle East, either. 'Saddam Hussein?' she said. 'He's a boxer, ain't he?'

Jade, asked by Big Brother to name two vegetables: 'Strawberries and spuds.'

She then shared with the nation this little gem: 'What's a sparagus? Do you grow it?'

And she confessed she thought horseradish comes from horses . . . that a ferret was a sort of bird . . . and that croquet is played on horseback!

Jade on intelligence: 'I am intelligent, but I let myself down because I can't speak proper or spell.'

She then went on to prove it by saying: 'They were trying to use me as an escape goat.'

Jade had a rival in the dummy stakes. Helen Adams filled the *Big Brother* house with loads of nonsense, including this after three contestants had been evicted. She exclaimed: 'God! There are nine of us in here. It doesn't seem as many as at the start.'

On the eve of an eviction vote, she said: 'I'm worried that I look chubby. There'll be lots of pictures taken of me tomorrow if I'm the one to leave. I just won't eat anything tomorrow.'

Talking about Paul Daniels, she said: 'Yeah, you know Jack Daniels . . . he does all that magic stuff.'

Asked about things she liked to do, Helen did not blink an eyelid as she replied: 'I like blinking, I really do.'

Helen on matters sexual: 'I've heard that when men's willies are erect they are all the same size.'

And then a little more naivety when a male contestant told her: 'I keep having wet dreams and wake up covered.' Helen replied: 'Really? Covered in what?'

Standing in the *Big Brother* kitchen, she asked: 'Is the jelly cooked?'

The suggestion was that Helen might have been just as silly in her outside job as a hairdresser. Asked if she had ever made a mistake while doing a customer's hair, she admitted: 'Once I cut someone's necklace off.'

Then along came Chantelle, a chirpy Essex girl who was placed in the *Celebrity Big Brother* house as a pretend celebrity. When she came out three weeks later it was into the full glare of publicity and as a celebrity in her own right.

She had some classic moments out of the Jade Goody/Helen Adams school of stupidity. Quizzing George Galloway – busy bringing the House of Commons into disrepute – she said: 'You work in that place with the green seats, don'tcha?'

After basketball giant Dennis Rodman had boasted of bedding more than two thousand women, she gasped: 'Oh my God, that's more than one hundred. That's even more than five hundred!'

When Michael Barrymore jokingly introduced himself as a gynaecologist, she took him seriously and asked: 'What's one of them? Never heard of it.'

I would have told her: 'Ask your mum.'

I am reliably informed that since she left the *Big Brother* house, Jade Goody has earned more than three million pounds. Chantelle is well on her way to her first million.

So maybe it's me who's the idiot.

Along with many people, I thought it was a bit of planned publicity-seeking when the icon that is Jordan – at 34FF she's the 'Eyeful Tower' – flirted in the jungle with Australian singer Peter Andre.

But they proved they really had fallen in love on *I'm a Celebrity, Get Me Out of Here!* by taking it all the way to the altar,

'Oh my God', it's Chantelle, who emerged as an overnight celebrity in a *Big Brother* show that destroyed the dignity of House of Commons MP George Galloway. Chantelle is living the dream, while Galloway is trying to live down the nightmare.

and a wedding that made the David Beckham/Victoria Adams affair seem a landmark in good taste.

Jordan, aka Katie Price, had described Andre's manhood as 'an acorn' during their flirting in the jungle. Several weeks before their marriage they had a son – which goes to prove that out of small acorns big things really do grow. Look what happened when an acorn and an icon got it together!

Jordan has become one of the leaders of the new-style celebrity, famous for being famous. But at least she can send herself up: 'Some people may be famous for inventing a pencil sharpener. I'm famous for my tits.'

She is a walking advertisement for the wonders of silicon, and plays the publicity machine better than George Formby played the ukulele. I don't think the public ever get to see the real Jordan, and there could be a very clever, very calculating mind hidden behind the image of the dizzy, big-bosomed blonde.

Jordan has also managed to bitch herself into the headlines with stiletto-dagger quotes like this one about that other shy, retiring role model Posh Beckham: 'She's got a great-looking husband, a nice little boy and all the money in the world. She hasn't got the looks, but you can't have everything.'

Miaooow.

In a poll conducted by Channel Four in 2003, Jordan was named the second most annoying Brit alive. She was beaten into first place by Tony Blair (the distance was a pain in the neck), but she managed to keep pain-in-the-arse Maggie Thatcher in third place.

Jordan responded: 'What goes around, comes around – I'm a great believer in that, so eat your apple pie.'

I think she meant to say humble pie!

Portuguese transsexual Nadia Almada won *Big Brother 5*, collecting more than four million viewers' votes in the final week. Her one big pout came when she failed the spelling test on the word 'balloon'. She complained: 'We don't have f***ing double Ls and double Os in Portuguese . . . f***ing double Ls and Os, it's just not fair.'

Wonder how she would have got on with spelling 'what a load of bollocks'?

I bet she didn't complain about the load of noughts in her £63,000 winner's cheque!

Reality television reached a new low when Rebecca Loos – famous because of alleged leg-over activity with David

Beckham – had a hand, so to speak, in a controversial scene on Channel Five's *The Farm*.

Viewers were shown explicit footage of Ms Loos masturbating a pig as she collected semen that would be used to inseminate sows.

She pulled it off with great aplomb.

A spokesperson for the rest of the animals on the farm said after Ms Loos's loose behaviour: 'Why do pigs get all the fun?'

They were referred to George Orwell's *Animal Farm*: 'All animals are equal, but some are more equal than others.'

Mrs Mary 'Keep TV Clean' Whitehouse, often revolting when alive, must be revolving in her grave. Suddenly, from reality television we were heading for the borders of bestiality TV. Now there's an idea . . .

Keith Chegwin revealed all when he full-fronted a Channel Five reality game show called *Naked Jungle*. Contestants showed their bits and pieces as they swung and swam around the studio set. It should have been called *Cheggers Goes Stark Bonkers*. It was the most disturbing sight on television since Noel Edmonds showed his crinkley bottom.

Cheryl Baker, ex-Bucks Fizz (careful not to do a spoonerism with that) really went to the bottom of things on a reality show called *The Salon*. She allowed the cameras to show her having a colonic irrigation.

Reality television, my arse!

What they call reality television today used to be known as fly-on-the-wall. I can remember a BBC series way back in the 1970s called *The Family*, which made brief celebrities of the Wilkins family of Reading. The nation was shocked by the strong language and unscripted views, but compared with modern shows like *Wife Swap* it was as tame as watching a vicarage tea party.

There was one particular wife called Lizzy Bardsley who could turn you off marriage for life. Blimey, I'd rather jump in the Mersey wearing cement boots than swap her for my Rita.

She had the foulest mouth of any woman I've ever seen on the box, and she caused domestic chaos wherever she stepped. And the way he came across in the programme, her husband seemed in my opinion to be a lazy git who made Jim Royle seem positively dynamic.

It emerged that she was raking in a reported thirty-seven grand a year in benefits for them and their eight kids, which all led to an investigation by social services and Dizzy Lizzy got found guilty of fraud.

The producers thought it all made great telly, and the programme won a coveted Bafta.

I wouldn't have given it house-room.

Another little snippet from *Wife Swap* involved a lady called Becky. Reacting to criticism from another wife, she said: 'F*** off. My house is a shit tip. So what? I don't believe in rules. My kids do what they want. Slit your wrists, love, it will lower your blood pressure.'

It made my blood pressure go up. How can this pass for entertainment? Bring back *Andy Pandy*!

To be honest, I've lost track of just what constitutes a celebrity. For instance, will Monica Lewinsky go down in history as a celebrity or just a tart?

These are just a few of the classic lines that accompanied the scandal of Monica playing the harmonica with President Bill Clinton's weapon of mass distraction in the Oval Office . . .

An independent counsel looking into the affair announced in an official statement that Miss Lewinsky was being debriefed.

The counsel report said after the debriefing – and I am not making this up: 'A ray of sunshine was shining through the Oval Office window directly on Lewinsky's face while she performed oral sex to completion on the President. The President remarked about Lewinsky's beauty . . .'

Shortly after the story broke about Bill and Monica, she was involved in a minor road accident. It was reported that she had blown a tyre. 'Wow! The President must have been easy compared with that' was among the more tasteful one-liners flashing around the comedy circuit.

Discussing her weight loss through a special diet after the scandal had died down a little, Monica said on television: 'I control my weight by being selective about what I eat. I never put anything in my mouth that is bad for me.'

You couldn't make that one up.

A few years later the same Miss Lewinsky – now considered a 'celebrity' – hosted a new reality television show in which young lady contestants had to choose a date from a group of masked men. Monica (sitting behind rather than kneeling under a desk) was on hand to give advice as to which was the right type of man to select.

Silver-tongued chat show host Jay Leno came out with the cracker: 'Who better to give dating advice without seeing a man's face than Monica Lewinsky!'

He added: 'At this time of crisis in Iraq, wouldn't she be better employed overseas entertaining our troops?'

When publicising her show, Monica appeared on *Larry King Live*. David Letterman, another chat show host with a great line in cutting humour, said: 'Monica really liked being on Larry's show. She is turned on by anybody with a desk.'

Wishing Monica a happy twenty-eighth birthday, Letterman said: 'How time flies. It seems like only yesterday she was crawling around on the Oval Office floor.'

*Celebrity Love Island* took reality television to far-off Fiji. Pity it didn't stay there. Twelve single so-called celebrities tried to titillate viewers – yes, titillate them – with suggestive, below-the-belt conversations that were near the knuckle and often much lower in the anatomy. They went all the way to the South Pacific to show twelve people behaving as if they were on a boozy night out in Newcastle.

The reality did not stretch to letting the viewers know why in a tropical paradise island there seemed to be an ice floe running between co-hosts Patrick Kielty and Kelly Brook. It would have been more appropriate had they presented *The Frost Report*!

As the viewing figures plummeted to fewer than two million the desperate producers brought in sexy model Nikki Ziering to try to spice up the action. She made no secret of her assignment to try to bed a – and I use the word in its loosest sense – celebrity.

How low can you get? Ask Monica Lewinsky.

I have to admit disappointment that one planned reality television show was cancelled at the last minute. It could have been a real eye-opener. An American company had arranged to cover the day-to-day lives of Liza Minnelli and her then husband David Gest. Some time later it was reported that they were apparently in a marriage from hell. Gest sued Minnelli, his wife of just sixteen months, for $10 million, claiming that he was suffering from emotional and physical damage due to being continually beaten up by lovely Liza! That would have made reality television with the gloves off.

In Australia they have *Big Brother Uncut*, which features full-frontal nudity, unbleeped swear words, cameras in the showers and 'scenes of a sexual nature'. Trust the Aussies to want to know what's going on down under.

'Nasty Nick' Bateman was kicked out of the first *Big Brother* show for cheating. He cashed in on his infamy by writing an instruction book called *How to Be a Right Bastard*.

Lesson one: Tell Davina where to stick her microphone.

With the broadcast in America in 2000 of *Who Wants to Marry a Multimillionaire?*, reality television went up the aisle to a new peak in appalling taste. The two-hour programme featured a hidden 'multimillionaire' choosing a bride from a group of fifty women.

The contestants paraded around in bathing suits and the semifinalists answered questions (for example, 'How would you spend his money?'). It was a thoroughly degrading spectacle that many viewers admitted watching through their fingers while cringing with embarrassment.

In the climax to the show the woman selected by the 'multimillionaire' married him there and then in a live televised civil ceremony.

The programme seemed dedicated to the theory that people will do anything for money, but it all backfired on the producers. It was later reported that their 'multimillionaire' groom was the subject of a restraining order obtained in 1991 by an ex-fiancée who accused him of assaulting and threatening her. This forced the American network to cancel a rebroadcast of the original show and the planned production of further episodes.

Then the media reported that the couple – the forty-two-year-old groom and his selected thirty-four-year-old bride – never spent a moment alone together on their 'chaperoned honeymoon' in Barbados, and had agreed to annul their union without the act of consummation having taken place.

They should have changed the title to *The Bride and Doomed*.

Inspired by the rash of shows polluting our screens, I have come up with an idea for a reality television programme that I want to pitch to a production company. Let me run it by you, see what you think . . .

It's called *Big Daddy*, and we get a dozen strangers locked together in a hotel somewhere deep in the country. What they don't know is that the Big Daddy character whose voice they keep hearing is the real father of one of the hotel guests.

With me so far? There's more . . .

The Big Daddy does not know himself which of the twelve guests is his son or daughter. By a process of elimination – based on questions sent in by viewers – he finds out which of them was fathered by him during a one-night stand in his past.

We would advertise for women to admit which celebrity impregnated them during a one-nighter, and then invite the product of the union along to the hotel.

The sequel could be the celebrity defending himself against having to pay backdated paternity payments. *Big Daddy* would, relatively speaking, put *Big Brother* in the shade.

What d'you think? I am sure there's a television executive jumping around in excitement at the prospect of paying me a million or so pounds for this unique idea.

*Reality television, my arse!*

# You've gotta laugh

A blonde (let's call her Jade), a brunette (let's call her Jordan) and a redhead (Helen) were stuck on a far-off desert island in a reality television show. All the viewers had switched off, and the production team had gone home, leaving the girls to die of boredom.

One day they found a magic lamp. They rubbed as hard as they could and eventually out popped a genie, who called himself Big Brother. He said that he could grant just three wishes, one for each girl.

Jordan went first. 'I hate it here,' she said. 'It's too hot and boring, and I'm missing Pete. I want to go home – right now!'

'Your wish is my command,' replied Big Brother. And off she went.

Then it was Helen's turn. 'I miss my family, my friends and the whole of Wales,' she wailed. 'I want to get out of this horrible place and go home to the land of my fathers.'

Big Brother bowed, and waved his arms. Helen disappeared home to Wales.

Jade, suddenly feeling lonely, broke down crying and said: 'I wish my friends were back here!'

# Hark who's talking about reality TV

**George Galloway:**
*(to Rula Lenska, Celebrity Big Brother, 2006)*
'Would you like me to be the cat?'

**Rula Lenska:**
'I'm a crazy Polish countess who likes a challenge.'

**Carol Thatcher:**
'I shall definitely always remember eating a squelching kangaroo testicle.'

**Tony Blackburn:**
'Wow! I'm the King of the Jungle.'

**Joe Pasquale:**
*(before being voted the new King of the Jungle)*
'Don't vote for me. I'm just a squeaky-voiced div.'

**John Lydon:**
*(aka Johnny Rotten)*
'The odds are we will all try to kill each other.'

**Janet Street-Porter:**
*(on dinner in the celebrity jungle camp)*
'It's like Christmas in a mental ward.'

**Natalie Appleton:**
*(the All Saint having a grumble in the jungle)*
'I'm not happy. Help me, help me please.'

**Paul Burrell:**
*(Talking in the jungle to fellow 'celebrity' Fran Cosgrave)*
'I wish I could offer you something to nibble.'

**Paul Burrell:**
*(still in the jungle)*
'The women are putting on make-up. They're washing their hair. Why don't we get time to do that?'

**Sheila Ferguson:**
*(going supremely over the top on her jungle experience)*
'It was very much like being in a World War Two concentration camp.'

**John McCririck:**
*(talking to 'blonde bombshell' Brigitte Nielsen in the* Celebrity Big Brother *house)*
'Your hair is awful. You have boy's hair. Cover that forehead up!'

**John McCririck:**
*(about to be booted out of the* Celebrity Big Brother *house)*
'I'm far too fat. Never employ a fat person. I'm eaten up by a desire for revenge. That's why I've got no friends.'

**Germaine Greer:**
*(just before walking out on the* Celebrity Big Brother *house)*
'I shouldn't have done it. I hate making mistakes.'

**Jack Dee:**
*(on his way to winning* Celebrity Big Brother, *2001)*
'Please, please, I'm begging you . . . vote me out of here.'

**Vanessa Feltz:**
*(who at one stage was shown scrawling gibberish on a tabletop)*
'I found the whole experience ridiculously intense and unnerving.'

**Jodie Marsh:**
'Is an egg a vegetable?'

**Traci Bingham:**
'What are we going to eat? Will there be food in the house?'

**Ozzy Osbourne:**
*(thinking aloud on* The Osbournes*)*
'It could be worse. I could have been Sting.'

**Rik Waller:**
*(talking about his near-thirty-stone bulk on* Celebrity Fit Club*)*
'It's not a big issue . . .'

**Michael Barrymore:**
'It's only a game . . .'

# 3 Do Not Adjust Your Set

Denis Norden (along with his clipboard) has entered the land of television legend as the presenter of *It'll Be Alright on the Night*, the daddy of out-take shows that has been on our screens since 1977. Those of a certain age will think that Denis has been with them all their viewing lives, and – as he is now well into his eighties – you can take it that he has been!

When I was first getting my ears around wireless humour, Denis and his long-time writing partner Frank Muir were in full flow with the classic comedy series *Take It from Here*, in which Jimmy Edwards, June Whitfield and Dick Bentley got laughs by the bucketful. That ran from the 1940s into the 1960s, and Muir and Norden were established giants in the comedy world long before Denis first started trawling through footage to find the most embarrassing television moments.

Until Denis started sniffing around like a bloodhound, fluffs and blunders by professional actors, TV presenters, weather forecasters and newsreaders were swept under the editing-room carpet and usually hidden from public gaze. Now everybody is on goof-and-blooper watch, and *It'll Be Alright on the Night* has spawned dozens of copy-cat shows that rattle skeletons in the cupboards of a procession of television performers.

Denis is big enough to put himself down while gently poking fun at foot-in-the-mouth actors and presenters. He tells the lovely story of the day a couple of winters ago when he got trapped in a horrendous traffic jam that brought London to the brink of grid-lock.

Desperate for a pee, Denis bolted from his jammed car to a side alley and – to his great relief – did his business against a wall. Just as he pulled up his zipper and prepared to dash back to his car a man opened his front door – obviously having watched him peeing – and shouted: 'Oi, I know you. You're that geezer off the telly . . . Barry Norman.'

'Er, yes, that's me,' agreed Denis, and then ran back to his car before he could be asked for an autograph or to explain his wall-watering performance.

The next day he telephoned Barry and told him: 'Sorry, mate, but somewhere in west London I've given you the reputation of being a bit of a flasher!'

*It'll Be Alright on the Night* has gained such a reputation as the home of gaffes that when we actors make the inevitable cock-ups we often say, 'There's another one for the Denis Norden collection.'

I am notorious for pulling doors that should be pushed, for my spoonerisms ('he fills her soul with hope' once became 'he fills her hole with soap'), and if there's a camera cable to be tripped over or a piece of furniture to be bumped into I will find them.

When acting in a series, I am a stickler for routine. As Jim Royle, for example, I insisted that the wardrobe department did not touch his trademark jeans and striped sweater from beginning to end. When I took them off at the end of an episode, I demanded that they be left in a steaming heap. I wanted to smell like the slob I was playing. If smelly vision had been invented, I think I would have proved a big turn off.

One of my most satisfying television jobs was appearing on *Cracker* with that marvellous, man-mountain of an actor Robbie Coltrane. A perfectionist on set, he was hilarious once the scene was safely in the can. We were continually falling about at each other's jokes. Here's an example of one of his: 'Did you hear about

This was taken during a break from shooting *Cracker* with that uniquely talented Scottish actor Robbie Coltrane. He takes his acting deadly seriously, but once the camera is switched off he becomes a walking mountain of mirth. He has an incredibly quick mind, and – for his funniest jokes – for some reason switches to awfully posh English.

the woman who went into the cocktail bar? The barman says, "What will you have?" She says, "I think I'll have a Double Entendre." So he gave her one.'

We went on location to Hong Kong for one of the episodes – 'White Ghost' – and during a break in filming Robbie and I passed the time with a walk through a local market. We stood watching a group of carpenters hammering, sawing and gluing before suddenly realising that they were coffin-makers.

They took one look at the two of us – me seventeen stone, Robbie around twenty stone – and shook their heads. An interpreter told us: 'They say they do not have enough wood in the whole of Hong Kong to accommodate you!'

Robbie is a brilliant mimic, and can pick up somebody's accent and imitate it within seconds. During the making of *Cracker* if ever the director shouted 'cut' because of a cock-up or a technical hitch he would suddenly switch from his Fitz voice to that of an awfully posh English wing commander in the RAF. 'Scramble, chaps,' he'd say, stroking a non-existent handlebar moustache. 'Ginger and Biffo have just bought it over the Channel.'

That's the beauty of recording for television. If you make a mess of a scene you can start again. But in the early days of BBC TV drama the plays used to be shown 'live' because there was no such thing as recording tape.

Veteran television director Ian Little-Smith tells this story that may literally rattle a skeleton: 'During a Sunday night play on the BBC in the early 1950s one of the supporting cast died on set – not dried, actually died – and the rest of the actors carried on, stepping over his body and sharing out his lines. During the famous pottery wheel interlude, while viewers made their cups of tea and waited for the second act, the body was removed from the set and the show went on!'

I've died on my arse a few times, but that beats them all. It's one out-take that even Denis Norden would not have dared show.

And here are a few more unscripted television moments that capture the unpredictable and at times crazy side of the business . . .

Tony Hancock could not remember his lines for 'The Blood Donor', one of the most famous and funniest comedy episodes in television history. ('A pint? Why, that's very nearly an armful.') He had banged his head in a car crash on the eve of the 1960s show, and was suffering from amnesia. Scriptwriting partners Ray Galton and Alan Simpson hurriedly organised a teleprompter, rarely used in those days. When you watch the episode again, notice how Hancock seems to be staring into space rather than at the supporting cast members. He is actually focusing on the teleprompter ready for his next line. Hancock had produced a masterpiece . . . but he could recall little about it.

Larry Hagman was forever plotting practical jokes on the set of *Dallas*, where he played his alter ego as the conniving J. R. Ewing. Just before rehearsing a love scene with his screen wife Sue-Ellen (Linda Gray) he rubbed liquid Procaine (a numbing substance used by dentists) on his lips. Both he and Linda spent the next hour drooling, with their lips out of control.

Linda was just recovering and preparing to shoot the scene again when Patrick Duffy (Bobby Ewing) came into the bedroom wearing swimming trunks, with a rolled-up football sock tucked inside them. He looked like a Very Big Man from Atlantis. Linda lost it completely and the director abandoned the rehearsal with the entire cast and crew in hysterics.

The wildly eccentric Hagman says that when he dies he wants his friends to eat him. He instructed his lawyer: 'I want to be fed through a wood chipper over a wheatfield, then have a cake baked from the crop, and slices sent to all my pals.'

I get indigestion just thinking of it.

Talking of indigestion, surely the television companies have reached boiling point with cookery shows. Bloody hell, you can't switch on the box without finding somebody fannying about in the kitchen. I use the word 'fannying' deliberately because it reminds me of one of the funniest unintended things I ever heard on television. David Coleman (of *Private Eye*'s *Colemanballs* fame) was introducing *Match of the Day* immediately after a show featuring the high priestess of the kitchen, Fanny Craddock. He came out with the classic: 'And for those of you who watched the last programme, I hope all your doughnuts turn out like Fanny's.'

Priceless.

Gordon Ramsay has managed to bring a touch of the unexpected and at times the horrific to TV cooking. He was so enraged when his Caesar salad was criticised by *Kitchen Nightmares* restaurateur Neil Farrell that he invited him into the restaurant's car park for a punch-up. They should have challenged each other to ladles at dawn.

Gordon literally swears by his skill in the kitchen. The nearest Fanny Craddock used to get to lord-mayoring was to say 'oh, bother' when monocled husband Johnny spilled the wine.

In *Kitchen Nightmares*, Gordon brought a trainee chef to tears and put him off cooking for life when he told him: 'This is a f\*\*\*ing nightmare. You are a lazy slob who lacks inspiration and your cooking is the f\*\*\*ing pits. It is an embarrassment to catering.'

Why does this man not say what he means?

He got his comeuppance when actress Amanda Barrie, another who had been brought to tears by his vicious tongue, slapped him after he had called her cooking crap. Well, Amanda has played a slapper a few times during her career.

Gordon Ramsay, Jamie Oliver, Antony Worrall Thompson, Keith Floyd, Rick Stein, Gary Rhodes, James Martin and the rest of the chef crew (there are enough to form a catering corps) are following in the slipstream of the Galloping Gourmet, Graham Kerr. He was a London-born, New Zealand-raised chef who used to race around the kitchen, always taking 'a little slurp of wine' and hurdling over kitchen stools and making risqué innuendo remarks while stuffing turkey and heating meatballs. He became an alcoholic, recovered and then turned to God and healthy food. Suddenly all the excitement and edge went out of his show, but he had found inner peace. He had become the born-again gourmet.

There may be too many well-grilled cooks spoiling the TV broth today, but they provide better telly than in the old black-and-white era when pioneer TV chef Philip Harbin used to say things like: 'And today I will be teaching you how to cook and then dress a lobster.'

Many of us on Merseyside watching this pompous prat were close to starvation rations and considered scouse stew a luxury meal. How to dress a lobster, my arse!

Delia Smith, who has always had a demure, dignified image as a sort of Queen Mum of the kitchen, astonished television viewers during the half-time interval of Norwich City's home match against Manchester City in 2005. A director of the Canaries, she came down on to the pitch, took the microphone and then yelled like a terrace yob: 'We need a twelfth man here. Where are you . . . where are you? Let's be 'aving you! Come on . .'

It was like walking into a room and finding Julie Andrews making a porn movie. Yes, it was that big a shock to the system. It made me wonder if Delia had been at the cooking sherry. But instead of making her a laughing stock (or a beef stock), she became a cult figure and Norwich City shirts carrying the 'Let's be 'aving you' slogan sold like, uh, hot cakes.

Comedy actor Leslie Nielsen caused quite a stink on GMTV when he loudly farted during a live interview. It was first of all greeted by embarrassed looks, then suppressed giggles and finally shrieking, uncontrollable laughter. They had to cut away to weathergirl Sally Meen on location. She said: 'It is also quite windy here.'

A few weeks later I was in Spain watching the local morning television programme, and there was Nielsen again letting rip, with similar reactions.

I then discovered that Nielsen is a serial farter, who has dropped noisy ones in television studios across the world. Just recently he confessed that he carries a fart button with him, and presses it whenever he thinks an interview is becoming too dull and serious.

I wonder if a few politicians should borrow it from him to liven up debates in the Commons and on political talk shows. Or do we have enough old farts on the backbenches?

*Baywatch* was always worth a look for a laugh, even though the show had its knockers. There was one particular episode when a pregnant woman went into labour on the beach. Lifeguard Mitch was the only one around, and he managed to deliver the baby single-handed. It was something of a miracle birth because the woman's bathing suit was on at the beginning and end of the scene.

In an episode of *Bad Girls*, a guard slams the cell door shut and the surrounding wall – allegedly stone – wobbles like jelly on a plate.

There was a similar scene in *Fawlty Towers* during the famous 'Kipper and the Corpse' episode. Basil pushed Sybil into the bedroom and slammed the door shut, and the walls either side suddenly bulged and threatened to fall in. John Cleese brought shrieks of laughter from the audience as he started to do his surveyor knock-knock routine, checking for weakness in the walls.

*Blackadder* remains one of the greatest comedy series ever produced anywhere, and is a prime example of British comedy acting and writing at its best. There was also some unintended comedy. In the second series, Edmund collides with a castle wall and the supposedly stone wall visibly shakes. More BBC plywood!

Sharp-eyed and well-informed viewers of the third *Blackadder* series noticed that the Duke of Wellington challenged the Prince Regent to a duel long before he was given his title. He was Sir Arthur Wellesley until 1814, the year before the Battle of Waterloo. The scriptwriters (Ben Elton and Richard Curtis) were obviously blessed with foresight and hindsight!

*Frasier* is not only one of the best comedy shows ever, it also provides proof that there is life after death. When he was a regular in *Cheers*, Frasier used to talk in the bar about his late father. In the spin-off series – moving from Boston to Seattle – his father Martin (British-born actor John Mahoney) comes to live with him. Miracle!

*Cheers* was famous as the bar 'where everybody knows your name'.

Bill Tarmey, a legend of *Coronation Street* as Jack Duckworth, could have made it big as a comedian or singer. When I suggested his on-screen character loves his beer more than he loves his wife Vera, he said: 'Jack loves his pigeons more than he loves Vera!'

In one episode Frasier shouts to bar owner Sam Malone: 'Get to the piano quick, Ted.' Of course, the actor who played Sam is Ted Danson.

*Coronation Street*, the peerless pioneering soap, does not escape the attention of the goof watchers. In the episode when Candice and Vik are going out together there is a romantic moment in their car. Careful scrutiny shows they were not alone. There is a reflection in the mirror of the cameraman sitting on the back seat. Anyone for a threesome?

In a made-for-TV movie about the life and times of Elvis Presley, there is a panning shot of the Mississippi territory where he spent his early days. Clearly seen on the wall of the house behind the young Elvis is a satellite dish.

There is a growing army of fanatics who use slow-motion action replays to spot cock-ups in television shows. *Bottom*, surely the most manic comedy series ever made, came under the microscope, and an editing goof was spotted in the 'Gas' episode. After Eddie Hitler (Adrian Edmondson) and Ritchie Rich (Rik Mayall) have bashed the gasman to death with a frying pan, Eddie panics and puts the pan into the dead man's hands. In the next shot, Eddie is holding the pan again.

Not the sort of thing most people would have spotted, but there are now a lot of 'TV detectives' who spend hours looking for goofs. I wonder if they should get themselves a life?

*Friends* attracted most attention from the goof ghouls, and these were the top mistakes noted:

- In the episode where Joey is going to be a butt double for Al Pacino he gets into the shower supposedly naked. His shadow on the wall shows that he is wearing boxers. The big wuss.
- In the first couple of episodes, Chandler and Joey's apartment was 4 and Monica and Rachel's 5. Both apartments had window views looking down from several storeys up. After eagle-eyed viewers pointed this out the numbers in later episodes were changed to the more likely 19 and 20.
- Monica said that she was cooking lasagne, then reached out and picked up a packet of noodles.
- Joey and Chandler were standing together in their kitchen during one early episode, and viewers noticed one fairly vital thing that was missing. It had everything *but* the kitchen sink!
- Phoebe got pregnant in January, and gave birth to perfectly healthy triplets in June.

A Sunday tabloid lifted the lid on the secrets of the modern version of *What's My Line?* and revealed – as if we didn't know – that the panellists were often fed the occupations of the guests before the show. Some could handle the information in a more convincing way than others.

Once, with Angela Rippon in the presenter's chair, the panel were getting nowhere near the occupation of a woman who had mimed how she stuffed teddy bears for a living.

There had not been the slightest hint of what she did when suddenly one of the panellists – I will protect his identity to save his embarrassment – said from out of nowhere: 'So this teddy bear you're stuffing in your mime . . .'

Everybody was stunned by this out-of-the-blue revelation. Angela Rippon recovered from her initial shock and shouted: 'Good heavens, he's got it . . . he's got it. What an incredible guess.'

Ernie Wise once 'guessed' an occupation without any clues whatsoever, apart from the mime. He just suddenly blurted out the right answer. The Sunday newspaper exposé revealed that he had been given the answer the night before the show. The producers just wished he had kept it to himself a little longer.

Has there ever been anything more toe-curlingly embarrassing on television than *It's a Royal Knockout*, which was the 1987 brainchild of Prince Edward and featured his sister Princess Anne, the Duke and Duchess of York and himself as team captains. It was all done in the name of charity. Many of us would have given a big donation to keep it off our screens. Prince Edward went into a sulk and walked out on a press conference because the hard-bitten, cynical journos would not say they had enjoyed it. This provided the only worthwhile footage from the whole sorry affair and his undignified exit still pops up on TV blooper shows nearly twenty years later.

Rivalling even *It's a Royal Knockout* in the embarrassment stakes was the dummy double act produced by former Page 3 girl Samantha Fox and Fleetwood Mac's Mick Fleetwood when hosting the 1989 *Brit Awards* show. It all got off to a good start when tiny Sam went to tall Mick's microphone, and he crouched to try to talk into her mic. It was like something out of *Monty Python* and unintentionally provided some of the funniest moments in TV pop music history.

They continually fluffed their lines, guests arrived late and often seeming in another world. A pre-recorded message from Michael Jackson went missing and a Bros video was hastily tacked on at the end when the show ran under time.

One of the most memorable moments came when Fox and Fleetwood over-talked each other while introducing The Four Tops, only for Boy George to walk out on stage. 'I'm afraid I'm just the one Top,' said a bemused George.

It was farcical . . . but television gold dust.

I thought Tom Cruise handled himself brilliantly when squirted with water from a fake microphone while giving what he thought was an interview at the premiere of his *War of the Worlds* film at Leicester Square in the summer of 2005. In this day and age of terrorism, that could have been acid or some poisonous liquid hitting him in the face. He stood his ground and said to the reporter, working for a Channel Four comedy show: 'Why would you do that? Tell me, why would you do that? You've been incredibly rude. Here am I being polite enough to give you an interview and you do that. You're a jerk.'

Deputy Prime Minister John Prescott, in a similar situation, retaliated with two stiff punches to an egg-throwing protestor's face. Two Jags suddenly became Two Jabs. In Tom Cruise's shoes I would have taken the Prescott route and hammered the idiot who squirted the water. And I would certainly have put my tongue to a stronger word than 'jerk'. I am all for a laugh, but not for taking the piss. The TV producer behind the prank showed a total lack of judgement.

When they tried the same water-squirting trick on Sharon Osbourne, she calmly walked into a nearby restaurant, picked up a bucket of ice, came back and chucked it all over the guilty cameraman!

I can almost hear Ozzy shouting, 'Good f***ing girl. That'll f***ing show 'em.'

The prat of a water-squirter was trying the same sort of interview approach as professional piss-taker Dennis Pennis, but was not in the same class for knowing how to get laughs. He made a fool of himself rather than the intended target.

Pennis, aka actor Paul Kaye, specialised in getting interviews with celebrities and trying to make them look stupid by asking ridiculously inane questions, or spouting one-liners at them to get a reaction. His self-styled description was 'media terrorist'.

He loitered outside film premieres and gala dinners, dressed as a punk, with dyed red hair and safety pins. With his thick horn-rimmed glasses and fake New York accent he was like a cross between Johnny Rotten and Woody Allen. Celebrities just did not know what to make of him, particularly as he was often holding a BBC-labelled microphone.

Pennis told a startled Pierce Brosnan after his first Bond movie: 'When I went to see *Goldeneye* I was glued to my seat . . . otherwise I would have left.'

To Dustin Hoffman, after he had starred as Captain Hook: 'Did you see the Tyson–Bruno fight?'

Hoffman looked at him blankly.

'It was just that you reminded me of Bruno. Neither of you could come up with a hook that people wanted to see.'

To Tom Hanks: 'Tom, I thought your new film *Apollo 13* was completely lacking in atmosphere.'

To Mel Gibson: 'In this film you play a hairy Neanderthal barbarian. As an Australian, aren't you in danger of becoming typecast?'

To Hugh Grant: 'You don't mind me telling you, I think you are a bit woody on screen. Do you prepare yourself by going to a forest and staring at trees.'

Hugh quickly realised he was being sent up and told him: 'You're a f***ing bastard.' The BBC bleeped his response.

To Jeremy Irons as he walked up the red carpet to a premiere: 'Jeremy, can I ask you a huge favour?'

'What's that?' asked Jeremy.

'Get out of my way, please' came the response.

He then walked right past Irons, leaving him looking totally bemused.

*Fawlty Towers* is one of the great untouchable classics of comedy, but it might have been considered even funnier if they had released an unedited version. The BBC have confined the out-takes to a DVD collection. John

John Cleese, who turned Basil Fawlty into one of the greatest of all television comedy creations. They made only twelve episodes of *Fawlty Towers*, and there have been so many repeat showings of the timeless classic that many of us know every line by heart. This was comedy acting at its very best. Whatever you do, don't mention the war!

Cleese has the audience breaking up with his gallery of hilarious Pythonesque poses as he glosses over cock-ups in his dialogue delivery.

Cleese scripted the two series in partnership with his then wife Connie Booth, who played the part of the hotel maid Polly. Just before the scene in which the deaf old bat complains about the view from her window ('What did you expect to see out of a Torquay hotel bedroom? Sydney Opera House, perhaps . . . the hanging gardens of Babylon . . .?') Polly gets the names of the guests muddled up and lets rip with the f*** word. You can almost hear the intake of breath from the audience. That would have caused an uproar if it had been broadcast during the 1970s when *Fawlty Towers* was recorded. Nobody – and certainly not a woman – could be seen or heard using that expletive on the box. How times change. When the BBC controversially screened *Jerry Springer, the Opera* in 2005 the show was peppered with hundreds of swear words. Just a thought: if *The Royle Family* had been made at the same time as *Fawlty Towers* there is no way Jim would have been allowed to say 'my arse'. Somehow, 'my backside' does not have the same ring to it.

Amazingly, the BBC considered not commissioning the *Fawlty Towers* series. That would have been an error of judgement to rank with turning down The Beatles. A memo sent by an executive to the Head of Light Entertainment read, 'This is a very boring sitcom idea. The script has nothing but clichéd characters and I cannot see anything but a disaster if we go ahead with it.'

*Fawlty Towers* got quite a whipping from the critics when the first couple of episodes hit the screen. The *Daily Mirror* led the way with the comment: 'Long John short on jokes.'

Now, thirty years on, it remains what many consider the finest and funniest British sitcom ever produced.

*Seinfeld* is one of the few sitcoms that regularly gets rated even better than *Fawlty Towers*. While the Cleese classic had a run of just twelve episodes, *Seinfeld* ran for nine seasons from 1990 and maintained an astonishingly high standard of comedy throughout.

A feature of the series was neighbour Kramer's aggressive

entrances into Jerry Seinfeld's apartment. Played by the brilliant physical comedy actor Michael Richards (a sort of talking Harpo Marx), he used to finish each episode bruised because of the way he threw himself around the set. In one episode he knocked himself out when he crashed his head against Jerry's door. Jerry, not realising he was hurt, tried to keep the scene going and said to Elaine (Julia Louis-Dreyfus): 'How is he?' She walked out into the hall and then casually came back into the apartment and announced: 'He's dead!' Shooting was delayed while Richards recovered . . . and to give the cast and crew time to stop laughing.

Jerry Seinfeld is in the *Guinness Book of Records* for turning down the biggest offer ever made to a television performer. He said 'no' to five million dollars an episode to make one more series in 1999.

Blimey. Most actors would have said 'yes' to five thousand dollars an episode. The world has gone barmy.

Serial bride Zsa Zsa Gabor was on television in America giving advice to viewers about how to handle problems of the heart. A young lady telephoned to discuss her broken engagement. 'My ex-fiancé gave me a mink coat, diamonds, a stove and a Chevrolet,' she said. 'Now that we're breaking up, what should I do with these gifts?'

Zsa Zsa had four words of advice for her: 'Give back the stove.'

It was Zsa Zsa, of course, who famously said: 'I have never hated a man enough to return his diamonds.'

Here's a true story that will take some topping, or toppling. Yorkshireman Bob Specas spent hours setting up 100,000 dominoes for an attempted world record knock-over in New York's Manhattan Center. It was due to be shown live on television, and the director asked his number-one cameraman how soon the push would be made. The cameraman leaned forward to look down from the balcony at the columns of dominoes below. 'The English guy is just putting the last ones up,' he reported, and as he said it his ID badge fell from his lapel, landed on the dominoes and set them off on a spectacular toppling chain . . . with poor Bob Specas looking on open-mouthed and rooted to the spot.

You cannot keep a good man down, though, and next Specas set off for Thailand. This time he was after the Thailand all-comers record for piling dominoes on top of each other. The local rules were that you had to drink five glasses of beer before starting, and the record to beat was 178. The venue: a bar in downtown Pattayaland.

Specas drank the specified amount of beer, and then set to work building the domino mountain. He comfortably reached 165 and then hit an unexpected problem. He had run out of dominoes. The bar owner sent a waitress to his office for an urgent extra supply, and when she returned she threw the bag of dominoes on to the table with such force that the Specas mountain came tumbling down.

I love a good cringe in front of the telly, and I have sorted out what I rate the Top 20 Most Embarrassing Moments involving celebrities on the box. See if you agree with my toe-curling choices. In time-honoured fashion, I announce the results in reverse order . . .

20. Richard Madeley making a right prat of himself when impersonating Ali G on ITV's *This Morning* show. No big up respec' 'cos it was terrible.
19. Neil Kinnock going arse over head on the beach at Brighton while walking with his wife, Glenys. Then his air-punching at the Sheffield meeting celebrating a victory that was about to be snatched from him. Kinnock was well and truly beached.
18. The Sex Pistols, led by Johnny Rotten, letting rip with a stream of foul language. I can lord-mayor it with the best of them, but swearing for swearing's sake is just juvenile. Mind you, interviewer Bill Grundy almost invited it. I half expected him to say, 'Make my day, punk!'

17. Glenn Hoddle and Chris Waddle dueting on *Top of the Pops*. What a load of twaddle from Waddle and Hoddle.

16. Chat show host Russell Harty getting slapped by singer Grace Jones because he turned his back on her. Disgraceful Jones.

15. The Gibb brothers walking out on Clive Anderson after he had made a throwaway 'tossers' joke about the Bee Gees on his BBC chat show. Not very brotherly, was it?

14. Robert Kilroy-Silk, Mr Tangerine Man, getting a bucketload of shit thrown over him by a protester as he arrived for a BBC radio show. What a waste of good shit.

13. Bobby Ewing coming back from the dead in Dallas and making nonsense of all the previous series' storylines. When he walked out of the shower the reputation of *Dallas* went down the drain.

12. Tara Palmer-Tomkinson out of her tree on *The Frank Skinner Show*. I don't know if she was boozed or what, but she came across as very dopey and not the sort of person you want in your front room. Frank should have said 'ta-ra, Tara'.

11. George Best, another booze victim, making an idiot of himself on Terry Wogan's chat show. The greatest footballer of them all humiliated himself. So sad.

10. Keith Chegwin showing his bits and pieces on Channel Five's *Naked Jungle*. I even covered the dog's eyes. There was not much to get excited about.

9. Politician John Redwood trying to pretend he knew the Welsh national anthem. It wiped out any hope of him getting a welcome in the hillsides.

8. Almost any *Eurovision Song Contest*, but particularly the 2003 show, when British entry Jemini scored 'nul points'. Jim Royle could have done better with his banjo, and the Beverley Sisters backing him.

7. At least twenty of the *X-Factor* hopefuls who should never have been allowed anywhere near a microphone, all of them making idiots of themselves on national television. How on earth do these people convince themselves they can sing? My cat could do better . . . and he's been neutered.

6. England football manager Graham Taylor setting a f***ing swearing record on the touchline on the way to defeat by Holland. What on earth possessed him to allow the production company to mic him up? He scored an own goal, and gave us a new catchphrase: 'Do I not like that.'

5. President Bill Clinton facing the camera and telling the world: 'I did not have sexual relations with that woman.' Blow me down, could you believe it?

4. That unforgettable night when Sam Fox and Mick Fleetwood brought us the long, short and the tall of embarrassing moments while presenting (in its loosest form) *The Brit Awards*.

3. England's footballers conceding a goal in a record nine seconds against the waiters and ice-cream sellers of San Marino in a World Cup qualifying match in 1993. I – along with many others – watched the rest of the game from behind the sofa.

2. The royal family making big bananas of themselves in *It's a Royal Knockout*. The Royle family would not have lowered themselves to take part, unless there were plenty of pies and pints as prizes.

1. It has to be the sickening sight of George Galloway, an elected Member of Parliament, purring like a cat while Rula Lenska stroked him during *Celebrity Big Brother*. This cat did not get the cream.

# You've gotta laugh

A veteran television actor was having trouble hearing the director's instructions, but he managed to ad-lib his way through the scene. He was surprised when it was announced that it would be shot again after a five-minute break.

As he came off the set, he whispered to the floor manager: 'Excuse me my man, but I let go a silent fart while delivering my last line. I hope it did not register with anybody.'

The floor manager told the director: 'I've realised the problem. He needs a new battery in his hearing aid.'

# Hark who's talking about the box

**Sir David Frost:**
'Television is an invention that permits you to be entertained in your living room by people you wouldn't have in your home.'

**Frank Lloyd Wright:**
'Television: chewing gum for the eyes.'

**Gore Vidal:**
'Television is now so desperately hungry for material that they're scraping the top of the barrel.'

**President Richard Nixon:**
'No performance takes as much preparation as an off-the-cuff talk on TV.'

**Jack Paar:**
'I have never seen a bad television programme, because I refuse to. God gave me a mind, and a wrist that turns things off.'

**Noël Coward:**
'Time has convinced me of one thing. Television is for appearing on, not looking at.'

**Joey Adams:**
'If it weren't for the fact that the TV set and the refrigerator are so far apart, some of us wouldn't get any exercise at all.'

**Andrew Ross:**
'The smallest bookstore still contains more ideas of worth than have been presented in the entire history of television.'

**Sam Goldwyn:**
'Television has raised writing to a new low.'

**Anon:**
'Theatre is life. Cinema is art. Television is furniture.'

**John Barrow:**
'I have come to feeling about television the way I do about hamburgers: I eat a lot of hamburgers and I don't remember a single one of them.'

**Fred Allen:**
'Television is the triumph of machine over people.'

**Lee Loevinger:**
'Television is a golden goose that lays scrambled eggs; and it is futile and probably fatal to beat it for not laying caviar.'

**Anon:**
'The same media people who claim violence on TV doesn't influence people are perfectly willing to sell you advertising time.'

**Lily Tomlin:**
'If you read a lot of books, you're considered well read. But if you watch a lot of TV, you're not considered well viewed.'

**Woody Allen:**
'In Beverly Hills, they don't throw their garbage away – they make it into television shows.'

**Jason Love:**
'I could have been a doctor, but there were too many good shows on TV.'

**Malcolm Muggeridge:**
'I have had my television aerials removed. It is the moral equivalent of a prostate operation.'

**Al Boliska:**
'Do you realise if it weren't for Edison we'd be watching TV by candlelight?'

**Alfred Hitchcock:**
'Television has done much for psychiatry by spreading information about it, as well as contributing to the need for it.'

**Orson Welles:**
'I hate television. I hate it as much as peanuts. But I can't stop eating peanuts.'

**J. B. Priestley:**
'What compels you to stare, night after night, at all the glittering hokum that has been deliberately put together for you?'

**Edward R. Murrow:**
'Just because your voice reaches halfway around the world doesn't mean you are wiser than when it reached only to the end of the bar.'

**Art Buchwald:**
'Every time you think television has hit its lowest ebb, a new type of programme comes along to make you wonder where you thought the ebb was.'

**Alistair Cooke:**
'When television came roaring in after the Second World War they did a little school survey asking children which they preferred and why – television or radio. And there was this seven-year-old boy who said he preferred radio "because the pictures were better".'

**Alan Coren:**
'Television is more interesting than people. If it were not, we should have people standing in the corners of our rooms.'

**Stephen Fry:**
'I don't watch television. I think it destroys the art of talking about oneself.'

**Jerry Springer:**
'My show is the stupidest show on television. If you are watching it, get a life.'

**Groucho Marx:**
'I find television to be very educating. Every time somebody turns on the set, I go in the other room and read a book.'

**Anon:**
'I wish there were a knob on the TV to turn up the intelligence. There's a knob called "brightness", but that doesn't work.'

**Ernie Kovacs:**
'Television: a medium – so called because it is neither rare nor well done. '

**Paddy Chayevsky:**
'It's the menace that everyone loves to hate but can't seem to live without.'

**Richard Burton:**
'Television is an evil medium. It should never have been invented, but since we have to live with it, let's try to do something about it.'

**Sam Goldwyn:**
'Why should people pay good money to go out and see bad films when they can stay at home and see bad television for nothing?'

**Peter Ustinov:**
'Acting on television is like being asked by the captain to entertain the passengers while the ship goes down.'

**Homer Simpson:**
'Television! Teacher, mother, secret lover.'

# 4 The World's a Stage

My experience of treading the boards has been confined to master of ceremonies work, some stand-up comedy and an ongoing tour with my 'one man, two man' show (appearing as the armchair slob Jim Royle in the first half, and then as my cantankerous self after the interval). If I could have changed anything in my early life, I would have gone to drama school, and then learned the acting craft in our wonderful network of theatres.

But that might have robbed me of a natural, spontaneous style they can't teach you in class, and I wouldn't be able to plaster a ceiling quicker than Roger Bannister can run a mile (well, he is in his late seventies now).

I have always been fascinated by the theatre, but also a little intimidated. I cannot imagine myself having the patience for a long run, repeating the same lines day in and day out. When I said this to Sir John Mills, he replied: 'My dear boy, actors go on their knees and pray for a long run. Better to stand in the same place on the stage every night than stand in the same dole queue every week.'

That was typical of the sense Sir John always talked before his final curtain call at the age of ninety-seven. I was privileged to get to know him well in his later years, and I hold him up as an example of how *true* celebrities should carry themselves in public.

He was modest, dignified, always approachable and extremely amusing company – the archetypal English gentleman. The two of us becoming friends was a classic case of opposites attracting! Many of the anecdotes on the following pages are out of the Mills memory bank. He was a born storyteller who was continually regaling his companions with wonderful tales of the theatre, his first love, even though he did his major work on screen. 'A question of the wallet ruling the heart' was how he put it. I was surprised to find that he was a fan of *The Royle Family* and, in particular, my foul-mouthed character Jim Royle. 'My dodgy eyesight meant that I listened to it more than watched it on television,' he said. 'The dialogue crackled, and you had a really meaty part that you could get your teeth into.'

People tend to think of Sir John as a man solely of the movies, forgetting that he had a distinguished theatrical career, including a starring role as war hero T. E. Lawrence (of Arabia) on Broadway. I suggested that he might have found some of the foul language and crude behaviour from Jim Royle a little hard to take. 'Dear boy,' he said, 'I was once in a play with Johnny Gielgud and a young actor called Bob Hoskins in which we turned the Royal Court Theatre air blue every night. It was called *Veterans*, and as we met for the first rehearsal I said to Johnny, "The language is a bit ripe, don't you think?"

'"Frankly, my dear," said Johnny in that wonderfully dry way of his, 'I don't give a f***!"'

I have another close pal who has spent as much time as even Olivier and Gielgud on stage. Take a bow, Ken Dodd, my fellow Scouser from Knotty Ash who is without argument the funniest thing on two feet. If you have not sat through a marathon Doddy performance at the theatre you have not seen traditional British comedy at its finest and funniest. He rarely works a stage for less than four hours, and has been known to be given the keys to lock up the theatre because the staff want to get home.

Doddy has played several Shakespearean roles, including Malvolio in *Twelfth Night* and Yorick in Kenneth Branagh's movie

Ken Dodd has spent as much time on the stage as acting masters like Olivier, Gielgud and Guinness. One thing's for sure, he has got a lot more laughs! Doddy and I are good mates, and whenever he telephones me he says to Rita: 'Is Rickety there?' She does not have to ask who's on the line! Ken is a comedy genius and a Liverpool institution. He thinks I should be in one.

version of *Hamlet*. He has also lectured on stage at the RSC at Stratford-upon-Avon, with 'Shakespeare the humorist' as his theme. Yes, truly a tattyfilarious fellow of infinite jest.

A connoisseur of comedy, Doddy quotes Freud's observation that 'a laugh is a conservation of psychic energy'. He then points out in true Doddy style: 'The problem with Freud is that he never had to play the Glasgow Empire second house on a Friday night.'

I once asked Ken if he believed in safe sex. 'Of course I do, Rickety,' he said. 'I've got a handrail around the bed.'

This has got nothing to do with the theatre, but it does show how hilarious Doddy is on and off stage. He is the man with the face that launched a thousand quips, and with trademark teeth that he once insured for four million quid. When he was being stalked a few years back, I heard it said that the woman was only after his teeth. She was an ivory hunter.

But back to the main thrust of this chapter – the theatre. And I start with this cracker passed on to me by Sir John Mills . . .

Rehearsals for *Oedipus* at the National Theatre in 1968 were not going well. Lines had not been learned, and there was a serious lack of energy. The director, Peter Brook, decided he needed to instil a team spirit. He called the cast to a crisis meeting and stressed that he wasn't getting enough fire and passion from them.

Sitting in the stalls, he said: 'I want you all, one by one, to come on stage and say something – anything – that will really terrify me and motivate the entire cast.'

Each actor stepped forward to centre stage in turn and roared obscenities and threats mixed with words of hope and encouragement into the darkness. Peter Brook sat impassive and unmoved.

Finally, it was time for the rallying call of the star of the play, Sir John Gielgud. He sauntered to the front of the stage, took a languid draw from his cigarette and said: 'We open in two weeks!'

Richard Dreyfuss weirdly switched to the third person when sending a barely coded message to *The Producers* creator Mel Brooks as he struggled to settle into his role during rehearsals for the 2004 opening of the London run of the show. He said: 'Tell Mel Brooks this: "Please don't yell at Richard. Richard doesn't like to be yelled at. Let's have a relaxed and creative atmosphere. Richard thinks of this as fun, not business. Business is about bullying and being nasty and, if any of that is directed at him, he shuts down because he feels it's all his fault."'

Dreyfuss had been questioning his own ability to perform the singing and dancing demanded of the part in *The Producers* and had suggested people should not come to see the show until he'd had time to get his performance up to scratch.

Within a week he had pulled out of the show, blaming a recurring back problem.

While rehearsing for their roles in the West Hollywood Coast Theatre production of *Turnaround* in 2003, *Friends* star David Schwimmer and the beautiful Jamie Ray Newman approached a sexy scene in which Newman's character had to make a grab for Schwimmer's, uh, family jewels.

'We had been dancing around the actual grab for a couple of days,' Schwimmer recalled, 'and finally Roger Cubble, the director, said, "You know what, you're going to be doing this five nights a week in front of the audience. Come on . . . just go for it."

'So we were all ready to do the scene and I said, "Hold on one second, I just want to check something."'

Minutes later they rehearsed the scene. Newman made her grab and found that she had got hold of a large, hard cucumber that David had slipped inside his boxers.

Suddenly they were more than just friends!

The theatre is notorious for producing some serious drinkers. Actors often turn to the bottle for reasons varying from pressure to boredom, and from a confidence crutch to escapism. And many do it for the pure hell and pleasure of it! There is a never-ending queue of actors at places like the Priory, where they seek drying-out and psychological help.

I have heard dozens of stories linked to drink, and many of them feature the two Richards – Burton and Harris.

Early in his career Burton came under the wing of a fine actor called Wilfrid Lawson, who was as famous for his capacity for drink as his acting ability. Some years later, in 1962, they met by chance in a pub close to the Old Vic where Lawson was appearing as Button Moulder in *Peer Gynt*.

They enjoyed a reunion drink or three, and then Burton accepted Lawson's invitation to watch him in his matinée performance. As Burton took his seat, he was startled to find Lawson joining him. 'I'm not on in the early part,' the veteran actor said with a slur.

Some twenty minutes later Burton was surprised that Lawson was still sitting alongside him. Suddenly Lawson took in what was being said on stage, and he tapped Burton on the arm. 'You'll like this bit,' he said, with a drunken grin. 'This is where I come on.'

Burton once admitted to drinking a bottle of brandy during a performance of *Hamlet* on Broadway. Sobering up the next morning, he asked a fellow cast member: 'Did it show how much I'd drunk?'

'The only thing we noticed', came the reply, 'was that you played Hamlet in the last two acts as a raving homosexual.'

Starring in Brendan Behan's *The Quare Fellow* at the Stratford East Theatre in London, the young Richard Harris met up with his best friend – another rising actor called Peter O'Toole – for an after-show drink. Eight hours later they arrived back at their digs aboard a milk float. 'I've no idea where we've been but I think we've had a great time,' Harris told legendary Stratford East producer Joan Littlewood. 'I think you could say we were *two* quare fellows.'

Joan said, very prophetically: 'Richard will develop into a great actor, and he is going to make friends with a lot of barmen along the way.'

Richard made such friends with a bar owner in New York that he was put in charge one night while the owner went to a ball game. It was like putting a drunken clown in charge of a circus. 'I almost ruined the business in one mad night,' Harris recalled some years later. 'I was giving drinks away to customers because I could not bring myself to ask for their money. When I started getting the big film parts I sent the owner a cheque to make up for the night I gave all his booze away. I'm told it was one helluva night.'

On being asked what message he was trying to convey with his play *The Hostage*, hard-drinking playwright Brendan Behan roared: 'Message? Message? What the hell d'you think I am, a bloody postman?'

Back to the wonderful Wilfrid Lawson. He and a fellow thespian had a heavy liquid lunch before appearing in a matinée of *Richard III*. Lawson stumbled on as the king and was slurring his way through the opening soliloquy when a member of the audience shouted, 'You're drunk!' Summoning all the dignity he could muster, Lawson roughly stared in the direction of his heckler and said, 'You think *I'm* drunk? Wait till you see Buckingham!'

Another from the John Mills collection: 'I was playing Puck to Robert Helpmann's Oberon in *A Midsummer Night's Dream* at the Old Vic just before the war. During our first read through on stage Robert broke wind with ferocious force. The entire cast collapsed laughing.

'Finally we managed to compose ourselves, and Robert said to our director Tyrone Guthrie sitting in the stalls: "Where shall I pick it up from?" Back came Guthrie's response: "From the fart."'

While Robert Helpmann was touring the United States with the Royal Ballet Company in 1949 they staged *Sleeping Beauty* at a huge indoor sports arena. Helpmann was given the dressing-room usually occupied by the match officials. Applying his make-up, he had to climb on a table to get close enough to the only mirror in the room. As he was doing the intricate eye make-up with his face close to the mirror, the stage manager entered. 'Everything all right, Mr Helpmann?' he asked.

'Fine and dandy,' the dancer replied. 'But goodness knows how the referees manage.'

I am assured the following story is true, but I think it should go into the apocryphal category.

Early in her career a young actress – who was later to become renowned in Hollywood for her physical attributes rather than her acting ability – woodenly played the lead in *The Diary of Anne Frank* at an off-Broadway theatre.

Her performance was so abysmal that when the Nazi soldiers entered the Amsterdam house looking for her, somebody in the audience shouted: 'She's hiding in the attic.'

Now this, on the other hand, *is* a true story but I cannot identify the star because to this day he knows nothing about it.

A singing actor, playing a supporting role in a London musical, had made himself so unpopular among the stage hands with his egomaniacal moods that they got their revenge during every performance. For one of the major numbers in the show he had to stand under a rain barrel that showered water on him. The water tipping down on his head was always liberally mixed with urine happily provided by the crew.

Rita Tushingham is a Scouse lass we are very proud of in Liverpool. The star of *Dr Zhivago*, *The Girl with Green Eyes* and *The Knack*, Rita says that she always liked the sound of applause. So much so that as a child she would lock herself in the bathroom, flush the toilet and take a bow. She said the sound of the water rushing away was like applause to her.

Rita started her acting on stage at the Liverpool Playhouse. She was particularly good at revue, and would ad-lib freely. One night, she poked her tongue out at the front row of the audience. Unknown to her, in the front row that night was one Dame Sybil Thorndike. But, far from taking offence, the theatrical legend put her hand up and said loudly: 'That little girl is worth watching . . .'

A young unknown actor with the Bristol Old Vic called Peter O'Toole landed a debut walk-on part as a Georgian peasant in the Chekhov play *Uncle Vanya*. The script simply called for him to come on stage, announce, 'Dr Astroff, the horses are ready,' and exit. The ambitious O'Toole was determined to squeeze every ounce out of the part. He elected to play the peasant as a young Vladimir Lenin, bringing to the surface just a hint of proletarian resentment bubbling inside. On opening night, the audience was duly intrigued by the entry of the tall, willowy and very angry peasant who, turning to Dr Astroff, resonantly announced: 'Dr Horsey, the Astroffs are ready.'

Michael Caine's first stage role – as a policeman arresting the villain in the final moments of a play – finished in farce. He had just the one line to deliver ('Come along with me, sir'), but the dialogue deserted him as he realised the audience were roaring with laughter on his entrance. He had come on stage with his flies undone.

He drew more unintended laughs in a later appearance as Cathy's cruel brother Hindley in *Wuthering Heights*. The strapping, six-foot-two Caine had to allow himself to be thrashed by a diminutive and extremely effeminate Heathcliff. 'Now that really called for some acting,' recalled Sir Michael.

Asked about his debut appearance at the National Theatre, Sir Anthony Hopkins recalled: 'It was in Olivier's *Othello*. I was playing the messenger and I watched from the wings as Frank Finlay came on playing Iago and gave his first lines. I thought, "Oh yeah, I know that." I'd learned that as an audition piece. Anyway, my cue came up and I ran on stage and went straight into Iago's lines all over again. Oh dear. There were blank and shocked faces all around me before I delivered the messenger's lines.

'I went backstage afterwards and saw the stage manager, and she called me an idiot. She said, "You've got to go and see Sir Laurence. He's absolutely furious with you."

'I thought he was going to have me fired and I'd never work again. As I knocked on his dressing-room door I was very nervous. "Enter!" came the booming voice of the great man. He was taking his make-up off, and I mumbled, "I'm sorry about the uh . . . cock-up . . . I'm sorry about speaking Iago's lines."

'"Oh dear boy," he said, "I thought we were going to start the whole play all over again!"'

Keeping company with Olivier on and off stage paid dividends for Hopkins later in his career. The master impressionist was called in to dub the late Olivier's voice in several scenes when the classic film *Spartacus* was re-edited for a modern audience. See if you can spot the difference when it next pops up on the telly.

Hugely (and I do mean hugely) talented actor Richard Griffiths stopped a performance of *The History Boys* at the National Theatre to bollock a member of the audience whose mobile phone kept going off: 'I am asking you to stand up, leave this auditorium, and never, ever come back,' he told the offender.

There was a repeat scene a few months later when Richard was appearing in *Heroes* at Wyndham's. He angrily stopped the show again when a phone rang repeatedly in the penultimate scene: 'Could the person whose mobile phone it is please leave?' he demanded. When she got up to go, he stepped to the front of the stage and asked her, 'Is that it, or will it be ringing some more? The seven hundred and fifty people here would be fully justified in suing you for ruining their afternoon.'

Griffiths said afterwards: 'It was one of the last crucial scenes of the play and I had already had to restart the speech twice because her phone had gone off. I didn't say anything until the third time, when I just thought it was too much.

'I would like us to copy what they do in New York and fine anybody whose mobile goes off during a performance. Failing that, we could issue people with machetes and tell them to hack the mobiles to pieces.'

When a mobile rang during a performance of *The Iceman Cometh* at the Old Vic, artistic director Kevin Spacey stopped the show and said to the owner: 'Tell them we're busy.'

David Suchet chose to cope with an identical situation in a more subtle but equally humiliating way. A mobile belonging to a member of

**Norman Collier has been treading the boards as a comedian with a unique act for more than fifty years. His chicken walk and club chairman act with the cutting-out mic are comedy classics. Norman recalls an early appearance at a Midlands theatre when he made his exit on the wrong side and found himself facing a brick wall. The next act, a magician working with doves, was already on stage as he tried to creep across the back. When he made it to the opposite wings he had a splatter of bird's crap on his head!**

the audience rang three times in less than twenty minutes during a performance of *Man and Boy* at the Duchess Theatre. On the third occasion, Suchet suddenly stopped speaking mid-sentence, allowing the phone to ring on and on while he stared into the middle distance with a look of cold fury blended with disdain carved on his expressive face. Time stood still. The phone continued to ring.

Suchet's stare became even more hypnotic, even more angry, even more disdainful. You could have measured the chilling moments in fathoms. Eventually the ringing stopped. A half smile, and he seamlessly continued from the very syllable he'd left off at when the phone first rang.

The owner of the mobile must have felt about as tall as Tom Thumb.

I was not quite as subtle as Suchet when a mobile went off during my travelling 'Audience with . . .' show. I was in Jim Royle mode, and told the owner of the mobile to stick it up his arse.

Each to his own.

Back in the pre-mobile days, Robert Stephens was appearing in *The Seagull* at the Greenwich Theatre when he became irritated by a non-stop chattering coming from the direction of the front stalls. He was applauded by the audience when he stopped midway through his speech to ask the two women involved in the inconsiderate chat to conduct their conversation elsewhere.

Last word to the dreaded mobile. One went off on the first night of a West End play, and the hushed audience and the entire cast heard a woman in the stalls answer it. 'Hello?' she said in a hoarse whisper. 'I can't talk, I'm watching a play.' After a brief but meaningful pause, she continued: 'No, not very . . .'

The gifted Ned Sherrin is a walking, talking anthology of theatrical anecdotes. One of his classics revolves around Old Vic director Michael Bethnall, who complained to his cast that the crowd scenes in *Julius Caesar* lacked animation. After the next show he reassembled the cast and told them: 'I know that I asked you to stop muttering "rhubarb" and say something realistic. But I don't want a repetition of last night when I distinctly heard one of you leave the Forum crying, "Taxi!"'

Michael Green, in his excellent *Art of Coarse Acting* book, suggested spear carriers in *Julius Caesar* should get some atmospheric Latin passion into their work. Instead of the traditional 'rhubarb' he proposed that they should say 'rhubarbum'!

Jerry Hall's nude appearance as Mrs Robinson in the West End production of *The Graduate* failed to impress the gentlemen of the press. *Daily Express* theatre critic Robert Gore-Langton wrote: 'Frankly, it's a storm in an A-cup.'

*New York Times* drama critic Clive Barnes attended a play called *The Cupboard*. His one-word review in the next day's paper: 'Bare.'

Reflecting on the way he and most other critics savaged Peter O'Toole's *Macbeth* at the Old Vic, Sheridan Morley said: 'It was not as bad as many of us said, but rather worse. It was summed up by a man I overheard talking to his wife on the way out of the theatre: "Well, all I hope is that the dog has not been sick in the car."'

Groucho Marx: 'I didn't like the play, but then I saw it under adverse conditions – the curtain was up.'

Writer and humorist Robert Benchley once attended the premiere of a Broadway play that was mind-numbingly boring. During the slow second act a telephone began to ring on the unpopulated stage. 'I think that's for me,' Benchley declared from the stalls. He then rose from his seat and left the theatre.

George Bernard Shaw sent Winston Churchill a note inviting him to the 1923 debut performance of his play *Saint Joan,* starring Sybil Thorndike. He enclosed two tickets: 'One for yourself and one for a friend – if you have one.'

Churchill had a prior appointment and replied: 'I wonder if I might have tickets for the second night – if there is one.'

Alan Bennett, whose gentle, wry observations of life have made him one of the country's best-loved and most famous playwrights, recorded the following entry in his diary:

'Spent today auditioning boys at Her Majesty's [for *Forty Years On*]. In the afternoon, when we had been going for about an hour, there was a quavering voice from the Upper Circle. "Could you tell me when you are going to start, please?" It was an old lady who had come for the matinée of *Fiddler on the Roof* on the wrong day.'

Ray Galton, who with his writing partner Alan Simpson created the Hancock classics and *Steptoe & Son*, tells this story that captures the fickleness and moodiness of we actors:

'Harry [H. Corbett] came into the television studio and we said, "Great set, Harry", and he said, "Yes, wonderful", and he turned round and asked, "What are all those seats for?" and we said, "The audience."

'"Audience?" he said. "I shall have to rethink my entire performance."

'Oh God, an actor.'

Russell Crowe started his acting career touring Down Under with a travelling theatre company. He logged nearly five hundred performances as the transsexual transvestite Dr Frank-N-Furter in *The Rocky Horror Show*. During a rowdy performance in Sydney, a member of the audience called out, 'Nice legs, dearie!' Crowe spun around to face the man. 'You'll never make a transvestite, darling,' he shot back. 'There wouldn't be enough lipstick to go around your mouth.'

Crowe said later: 'I found out after the show that he was a genuine transvestite, and he insisted on buying me a beer.'

Robin Williams and Christopher Reeve studied under legendary acting teacher John Houseman at the famous Juilliard School in New York. 'We were sitting in his office,' Williams later recalled, 'because we were master students, and Houseman said, "Mister Williams, Mister Reeve, the theatre needs you. You will pride yourselves as apprentices and soldiers in the army of the theatre . . . unless, of course, you can make shitloads of cash making movies."'

Agatha Christie's *The Mousetrap* has been running since way back in 1952. Richard Attenborough played Detective Sergeant Trotter in the first seven hundred performances and recalled: 'When we were in Nottingham for a trial run of the play before coming to the West End all of us in the cast were worried that the second act did not seem to be working. We talked anxiously about it into the wee small hours, with Agatha Christie quietly sitting listening to our fears. Eventually she opted to go to bed. "I should stop worrying about it and get a good night's sleep," the great lady advised. "I think we might get quite a nice little run out of it."'

Comedian Bob Hope once told a New York theatre audience: 'The hotel room where I'm staying is so small that the rats are round-shouldered.' The humourless owner of the hotel threatened to sue.

Hope offered to retract the remark and said during a subsequent performance: 'I'm sorry I said that the rats in that hotel were round-shouldered. They're not.'

No collection of theatrical tales would be complete without a visit to the Master, Noël Coward. Here he is at his wittiest and most cutting . . .

- After watching a play written as a showpiece for a fourteen-year-old child prodigy – who was on stage throughout the three acts – Coward said: 'Two things should have been cut – the second act and that youngster's throat.'

- As he left the theatre after watching Anna Neagle at less than her best in the role of Queen Victoria in *Victoria Regina*, Coward said: 'I never realised before that Albert married beneath him.'

- During a rehearsal for the stage presentation of the *South Sea Bubble*, Claudette Colbert kept fluffing her lines. 'Oh damn,' she said to co-star Coward, 'I knew these lines backwards last night.'

- 'And that, my dear,' said Noël, 'is the way you are saying them this morning.'

- Hearing that Michael Redgrave and Dirk Bogarde were to star together in *The Sea Shall Not Have Them*, Coward said: 'I fail to see why not; everybody else has.'

- After watching Lionel Bart's flop musical *Blitz*, Coward said: 'It was as long as the real thing, and twice as noisy.'

- After spending time in the company of Henry Fonda and his wife: 'The Fondas lay on the evening like a damp mackintosh.'

- On opera: 'People are wrong when they say opera is not what it used to be. It is what it used to be. That is what's wrong with it.'

- On his drinking habit: 'I am not a heavy drinker. I can sometimes go for hours without touching a drop.'

- Summing up his famous wit: 'It isn't difficult, you know, to be witty or amusing when one has something to say that is destructive, but damned hard to be clever and quotable when you are singing someone's praises.'

Sir Alec Guinness was self-effacing and always quick to tell stories against himself, such as: 'I handed in my coat at a hotel cloakroom and offered to give the attendant my name, but was quite pleased and a little flattered to be told that it would not be necessary. The coat was later handed back to me with the ticket still attached and on it the inscription, "Bald with glasses."'

Sir Alec once returned a script with a polite rejection, and had his letter answered with the following plea: 'We tailored it just for you.'

'But', Guinness replied, 'no one came to take measurements.'

He had a long-term friendship with another knight of the stage,

Sir Ralph Richardson. 'For all our many hours together,' he recalled, 'I never really knew about any real beliefs he might have had apart from the mastery of motorbikes over motorcars and the preference of gin to whisky. But then on one occasion I got an unexpected insight to his soul when he suddenly rose to his feet after a liquid lunch, raised his glass in a military-style toast and announced: "To Jesus Christ, what a splendid chap!"'

Another wonderful anecdote about Ralph Richardson has been passed on to me. I have a feeling it may have been invented, but why let facts spoil a good story?

Ralph once spotted an old acquaintance in a theatre bar. 'My dear Chudleigh!' he cried. 'Goodness, how you've changed! You look so much younger, perhaps because you've shaved off that awful moustache, and I much prefer that hairstyle. And not a hint of grey, you lucky blighter.'

The bewildered man stared at Richardson. 'But my name isn't Chudleigh,' he remarked.

'What?' Richardson replied. 'Changed your name, too?'

Sir John Mills relayed this story that was handed down to him by his old friend Sir John Gielgud: 'There was an elderly theatregoer called Miss Pilgrim who was a regular at the Old Vic for years. She always sat in the gallery and at the end of the performance she would sing "God Save the King" in a very loud, cracked voice. She had distinctive half-moon glasses and would be the first to arrive and the last to leave. All the actors and theatre staff knew her by sight, and she used to write letters to everybody about little things she noticed in the plays.

'When Tyrone Guthrie took over the Old Vic direction, with stars like Charles Laughton, Athene Seyler, Flora Robson and James Mason in the company, Miss Pilgrim was not at all in favour. She considered him wrong for the job.

I was proud to have Sir John Mills as a friend in his later life. If you are going to measure celebrity on a scale of 1 to 10, he was a definite 10 out of 10. His career stretched for more than 70 years, and took in every branch of acting. A true gentleman of the stage and screen, and the instigator of several of the stories in this chapter.

'One night she went to the stage door and asked everyone to sign their autographs for her as they came out of the theatre.

'A few days later they discovered that the paper had been folded over and on the other side she had written a demand to the Governors that Tyrone Guthrie should be sacked. And it was signed as a round robin from the cast!'

I finish my trawl of theatre tales with a collection of Sir John Gielgud's famous gaffes that made him much loved by the acting fraternity. He himself said: 'I've dropped enough bricks to build another Great Wall of China' . . .

Attempting to start a conversation with Prime Minister Clement Attlee at a banquet: 'Tell me, where are you living now?'

Trying to give words of encouragement to his friend Alec Guinness: 'My dear boy, why on earth do you want to try to take on the big parts when you do the little people so well?'

On seeing Christopher Reeve, who was walking through a film studio canteen wearing a full Superman outfit: 'Christopher, Christopher, I quite forgot to ask. What are you doing now?'

After seeing Richard Burton's *Hamlet*, he remarked to Elizabeth Taylor: 'I don't know what happened to Burton. I think he married some terrible film star and had to live abroad.'

He went to see Burton in his dressing-room after his *Hamlet* performance meaning to say: 'We'll go to dinner when you're ready.' It came out as: 'We'll go to dinner when you're better.'

At a dinner party, he described an actress as being 'as dreadful as poor, dear Athene on a very bad night'. Unfortunately, Athene was sitting right opposite him. Gielgud's attempt to back-pedal was hardly convincing: 'Not you, Athene. No, of course not, another Athene entirely.'

When at a dress rehearsal of his production of Mozart's *Don Giovanni* at Covent Garden, there was a technical hitch, he shouted: 'Oh stop, stop, stop! Do stop that dreadful music!'

While preparing to give his acclaimed performance as Dudley Moore's man-servant in *Arthur*, he overheard Dudley playing the piano in the studio (he was one of Britain's greatest jazz pianists before concentrating on his acting career). Sir John, intending to praise his talent at the piano rather than denigrate his acting ability, said: 'Goodness me, dear boy, you should have stuck to piano playing.'

# You've gotta laugh

A pal of mine – let's call him Trevor – had been in the theatrical business for years, as a scene shifter doubling up as non-talking extra for dozens of plays. His big ambition was to get a speaking part, and one day his dream came true. When an actor cried off at the last minute on the eve of opening night the director gave him a line in a play about the Battle of Waterloo.

He was to play one of Wellington's guards, coming on from the wings to declare: 'Hark, sir, the sound of cannon.'

He went home that evening and practised the line over and over again in front of the mirror. 'Hark, sir, the sound of cannon.'

Trevor tried it in a variety of accents, and with different resonance to his voice. He finally decided to play safe and stick to his native Scouse accent: 'Hark, sir, the sound of cannon.'

On the way to the theatre he got stuck in an almighty traffic jam that gridlocked Liverpool, and so he missed the dress rehearsal. He would have to go into it cold.

The tension started to grip him as he sat in his stationary car. 'Hark, sound, the sir of cannon.'

Now panic set in. He could not remember the line. 'Hark, cannon, the sound of sir.'

He was sweating buckets by the time he got to the theatre, but a sudden calmness descended on him when he put on the guardsman's uniform for the first time. It was as if he were now made to measure for the part, and he actually felt he was one of Wellington's gallant men.

On cue he came racing urgently from the wings, and as he reached centre stage the sound-effects men played the tape that sent the booming report of a cannon around the theatre.

Trevor jumped a mile in the air and shouted: 'What the f*** was that?'

# Hark who's talking about acting

**Roger Moore:**
'Some are blessed with musical ability, others with good looks. Myself, I was blessed with modesty . . . I enjoy being a highly overpaid actor.'

**Jack Carson:**
'A fan club is a group of people who tell an actor he's not alone in the way he feels about himself!'

**Elizabeth Taylor:**
'Some of my best leading men have been horses and dogs.'

**Robert Mitchum:**
'Some of my leading women have been dogs.'

**John Osborne:**
'Don't clap too hard. This is a very old building.'

**Patrick Stewart:**
'One day, out of irritation, I said, "You know all of those years with the Royal Shakespeare Company, all those years of playing kings and princes and speaking blank verse, and bestriding the landscape of England, was nothing but a preparation for sitting in the captain's chair of the *Enterprise*."'

**Sir Ben Kingsley:**
'I think the cinema you like has more to do with silence, and the theatre you like has more to do with language.'

**Glenda Jackson:**
'The important thing in acting is to be able to laugh and cry. If I have to cry, I think of my sex life. If I have to laugh, I think of my sex life.'

**Tallulah Bankhead:**
*(on being shown a script for a new play)*
'There is less in this than meets the eye.'

**Dorothy Parker:**
'The only thing I didn't like about *The Barretts of Wimpole Street* was the play.'

**Oscar Wilde:**
*(after the first performance of his play* Lady Windermere's Fan*)*
'The play was a great success, but the audience was a total failure.'

**James Cagney:**
'One of my early parts on the stage was in a show called *Every Sailor* and I had fun doing it. But I struggled to tell my mother. She didn't approve at all. You see, I played a chorus girl.'

**Helen Mirren:**
'When you do Shakespeare they think you must be intelligent because they think you understand what you're saying.'

**Nicolas Cage:**
'There's a fine line between the method actor and the schizophrenic.'

**Sir John Gielgud:**
'There's life for an actor in the characters he plays. Being another character is more interesting than being yourself. It's such a beautiful physical escape.'

**Paul Scofield:**
'The actor should make you forget the existence of author and director, and even forget the actor.'

**Richard Attenborough:**
'At my age the only problem is with remembering names. When I call everyone darling, it has damn all to do with passionately adoring them, but I know I'm safe calling them that. Although, of course, I adore them too.'

**Tom Baker:**
'Actors are able to trick themselves into treating anything as if it's fantastic. It's a kind of madness really.'

**Richard Burton:**
'When I played drunks on stage I had to remain sober because I didn't know how to play them when I was drunk. Yet I could play sober people with a lot of drink inside me, and nobody would be any the wiser.'

**Michael Caine:**
'The best research for playing a drunk is being a British actor for twenty years.'

**Charles Dance:**
'I was a window dresser for Burton's once while resting. What really put me off was the area manager coming round and saying, "Charles, I think you're a natch at this."'

**Christopher Ecclestone:**
'I think theatre is by far the most rewarding experience for an actor. You get four weeks to rehearse your character and then at 7.30 p.m. you start acting and nobody stops you, acting with your entire soul.'

**Leonardo DiCaprio:**
'Don't think for a moment that I'm really like any of the characters I've played. I'm not. That's why it's called "acting".'

# 5 A Corps of Corpsers

I confess to being a born giggler, and have cost television and film companies valuable time because of my tendency to fall about laughing in the wrong places. In the trade we call it corpsing, and over the next few pages I am going to expose the kings and queens of giggle.

But first I will give you a few instances when I have been the culprit who has brought production to a halt because of a failure to control my chuckle muscles.

During my happy days as Jim Royle I found a 'mirth mate' in Craig Cash, the co-creator of the series, who played the part of my son-in-law Dave. We could set each other off with out-of-script moments that threatened to hold the show up for ages while we tried to compose ourselves.

The vastly talented Caroline Aherne, the driving force of the show, who played my daughter Denise, used to tell us: 'Just don't look at each other.'

That used to make it all the worse as we tried to avoid our eyes meeting, and we would become convulsed with laughter. Then Caroline would be drawn into our net and she would lose it too. The three of us would finish up almost literally crying.

I remember one episode when Craig – watching the television from the sofa alongside Caroline – had to deliver the line, 'Oooh, that Helen Mirren . . . she don't mind flipping her tits out.'

For some reason he said, 'Oooh, that Helen Mirren . . . she don't mind flipping them.'

This completely threw me, and instead of responding with my line I started to giggle. That started Dave off, and our director shouted 'cut'.

After a few moments, we went for a second take, and again Craig said, 'Oooh, that Helen Mirren . . . she don't mind flipping them.'

That was it. I broke into uncontrollable laughter. Craig joined in, and so did the crew. The deadline-dictated director reluctantly had to tell us to 'take five'.

Some time later we were shooting another episode that featured my good mate Geoffrey Hughes, who won a place in the hearts of viewers with his performances as Eddie Yeats in *Coronation Street*. He was also a fat slob in an armchair as Onslow in *Keeping Up Appearances* before Jim Royle started his sit-in.

Geoffrey made an important contribution to the success of *The Royle Family* as Jim's best mucker, Twiggy. Many people considered the funniest scene in the series was when Geoffrey, Sue Johnston (playing Jim Royle's wife), Craig and I danced to the hugely rhythmic 'Mambo No. 5' while stripping wallpaper in the sitting-room.

It would have been even funnier if we'd shown the attempted first take. Geoffrey was wearing loose-fitting jeans, and as he boogied to the music they fell down to his ankles. He looked like a beached whale, and the entire cast and crew collapsed into helpless laughter as we took in the sight of his grey Y-fronts, which looked as if they had been bought in the 1960s.

The lovely Sue Johnston, an actress-and-a-half, said between gales of laughter: 'I thought it was only women who wore passion killers!'

Another of my laughter hold-ups came when I was making a pilot television show called *Ricky's Joke Shop*. I was playing the part of the proprietor of a shop selling new and slightly used gags, and I was telling the following golden oldie joke to that scally of a Scouse comedian Ted Robbins (nicknamed in the show the Thief of Bad Gags):

'A Sunday school teacher was talking to her pupils about life after death, and she asked the class: "How would you face up to passing on to the next world?" Little Tommy Jones put up his hand, and said: "I want to go like my grandfather, Miss, dying peacefully in my sleep . . . not screaming in terror like his passengers."'

Something you might not know is that I am a chronic asthmatic, and I had fought off an attack just before telling this joke. The result was that I was sounding like punctured bagpipes as I delivered the punchline, and Ted couldn't resist wickedly going off script.

'Are you the heavy breather who's been pestering my wife, pal?' he asked with a poker face. 'She's happy to keep taking your calls . . . but I object to you reversing the charges.'

It was a real show-stopper, and I laughed so hard that I couldn't get a word out for the next ten minutes. I could hardly catch my breath, and it had nothing to do with my asthma. Eventually the director, Brian Klein – laughing along with everybody else – had to tell us to take a break, while Ted and I regained some sort of control.

Ted, now establishing himself as a fine comedy actor after many years as the best warm-up man in the business, told me that if ever I worked with Peter Kay the show would never get finished.

He featured with the multi-talented Kay in *Phoenix Nights*, and recalled one scene that took thirty takes because Peter had his co-stars in hysterics with his ad-libs and a high-pitched laugh that was completely contagious.

But there is no argument about who is the Past President of the Gigglers' Club – another Peter . . . the one and only Peter Sellers.

He and Spike Milligan used to set each other off in *The Goon Show*, which for those of us of a certain age was compulsive

**The Kings of the Corpsers . . . Peter Sellers (left), Harry Secombe and Spike Milligan, pictured at a reunion of *The Goons*. They laughed almost as much as their audience.**

listening in the early post-war days of wireless entertainment. Years later Sellers revealed that if either of them started to get the giggles they would go back behind the stage curtain to stop their laughter being picked up by the microphones.

In one scene Harry Secombe (as Neddy Seagoon) let go with one of his famous raspberries that was so strong that spittle hit Sellers in the face. He and Spike collided as they dashed behind the curtain together, and while they were convulsed with laughter Harry valiantly carried on alone. As it was totally off-the-wall Goon humour, we listeners took it as normal that Neddy should be talking to himself.

Sellers was just serving his apprenticeship as a chronic corpser at that point and he features first in my collection of stories about a gaggle of gigglers . . .

In one of the *Revenge of the Pink Panther* scenes, Sellers was dressed in a fat suit, disguised as a mobster. He was in a crowded lift, and off-camera director Blake Edwards had told them all to imagine somebody had farted. After half a dozen takes that did not work, Sellers told Edwards that a farting noise would help conjure up the image. Edwards volunteered to make the noise, and the cast were then all supposed to stare ahead, trying to look innocent of the deed. It worked for a couple of seconds after Edwards had trumpeted, but Sellers slowly lost it and started crying with laughter. It took ages for the cast and crew to recover.

Remember the classic scene when Sellers is disguised as Toulouse-Lautrec, scurrying on his knees carrying a bomb ('a berm') that is about to explode? In one of the early takes the fuse went out, and Peter said: 'The berm, it is kaput.' He then laughed so much that director Blake Edwards ordered everybody off the set while he regained his composure.

Sellers was an obsessive perfectionist, and used to get himself in a right state wrestling with exactly how to get the best out of every second of a film. One particular *Pink Panther* scene was not working to his satisfaction, and he told Blake Edwards that he was going back to his hotel to sleep on it. In the middle of the night, Edwards got a phone call from an excited Sellers, who told him: 'I've just spoken to God and he's told me how to do it.'

On set the next day, even with divine help, the scene still did not work the way Sellers and Edwards wanted it to.

'Next time God gets in touch,' Edwards said, 'tell Him to stay out of the film business.'

Peter collapsed laughing yet again.

While making the cult film *Dr Strangelove*, Peter – in his role as US President (one of three parts he played in the film) – had to tell the Russian Premier that a nuclear bomb was being launched on Moscow.

Talking on the telephone, he improvised: 'I'm sorry, too, Dimitri . . . I'm very sorry . . . *All right*, you're sorrier than I am, but I am sorry as well . . . I am as sorry as you are, Dimitri! Don't say that you're more sorry than I am, because I'm capable of being just as sorry as you are . . . So we're both sorry, all right?! . . . All right.'

Director Stanley Kubrick said he had to stuff a handkerchief in his mouth to stop himself from laughing, but he and the entire crew went into apoplectic laughter in a later scene. As Dr Strangelove, Peter had a stiff right arm that was continually trying to break into a Nazi salute. Wrestling with the arm, Peter had the right hand around his throat and was pretending to throttle himself.

'It was pure comic brilliance,' said Kubrick. 'It took ages to get into the can because Peter kept giggling when he was meant to be gurgling!'

Dudley Moore could match Sellers and Milligan in the hysterical laughter stakes. Peter Cook revealed that it was always his evil intent to make Moore break up when they were performing their hilarious Pete and Dud sketches. 'Dudley knew that if I could catch his eye he had no chance,' Cook said. 'He would look at his feet, at the far wall and at his navel . . . anywhere to try to avoid my gaze.'

When they were sitting in a pub shooting the celebrated 'Greta Garbo' sketch ('It was bloody Greta Garbo knocking on my bedroom window . . .'), Cook managed to catch Dudley's eye. It is one of the funniest things ever seen on television, as Dudley almost bursts trying not to laugh.

They later shot an equally hilarious sketch when Pete philosophises on the meaning behind the nudes painted by Rubens. 'My Aunt Dolly was one of them artist's models,' says Dud. 'Yeah,' ad-libs Pete, 'your Aunt Dolly would do anything for nothing – dirty cow!' Dudley was eating a sandwich and later admitted he almost choked on it as he battled not to corpse.

Liza Minnelli, Moore's co-star in the two *Arthur* films, said: 'Dudley had a huge capacity to make people around him feel happy and laugh . . . and he also had a sometimes unfortunate knack of making *himself* laugh. The director continually had to order the cameras to be switched off because we were having screaming fits of laughter. Dudley and I would at last get ourselves calm and collected, and then a member of the crew would release a suppressed laugh and we would be off again. It was nothing unusual for us to have to shoot a scene as many as twenty times.'

Liza's mother, the legendary Judy Garland, was another eminent member of the corps of corpsers. In the scene in *The Wizard of Oz* when she slaps the supposedly ferocious lion (Bert Lahr) on screen we see her looking concerned when the lion starts to cry. In earlier takes, Judy had burst out laughing at the expressions on Lahr's face. She laughed so hard that it turned into hysterics. Director Victor Fleming slapped her face and sent her to her dressing-room to pull herself together. An hour later the scene was in the can, with Judy looking suitably sympathetic after slapping the lion's face.

The late, great master of mirth Ronnie Barker was another corpser. Lynda Baron, who played his long-suffering fiancée in *Open All Hours*, recalled that he had only to pull a face for her to start giggling. 'It got so bad during one episode', she said, 'that the director sent us home for the rest of the day like naughty children. The next day Ronnie said, "I won't giggle if you won't," which of course set us both off again and the director was not best pleased.'

During a tour of the chat shows, William Shatner revealed that the *Star Trek* actors were notorious for corpsing. He recalled one scene that needed several takes after Leonard Nimoy, playing the supposedly emotionless Mr Spock, was scripted to deliver the line: 'The plants act as a *repository*.' Instead he said: 'The plants act as a *suppository*.' Cue collapse of the entire *Star Trek* crew.

In another out-take, Shatner was supposed to be making a passionate speech from the bridge as Captain Kirk when he suddenly launched into a complaint about the food served in the studio canteen.

The biggest reason for hold-ups and corpsing was malfunctioning of the various sliding doors, and an entire morning's shoot was lost when an automatic door leading to the command module jammed with two of the cast inside. Houston, we have a problem . . . call the carpenters!

I can hardly leave the masters Morecambe and Wise out of my collection. They used to have everybody on their sets in stitches, and cameramen and sound engineers used to have aching ribs at the end of a shoot, much of it, I hasten to add, caused by Scouse scriptwriter Eddie Braben.

In one of the all-time great sketches with André Previn (Eric: 'I played all the right notes, but not necessarily in the right order . . .') the members of the orchestra could not keep straight faces, and finally the director decided they would have to go with it because he knew it would be pointless trying to tell them not to laugh. Previn said later that he had never hurt so much from laughing in his life.

Comic genius Tommy Cooper used to laugh at his own daft jokes ('. . . because I could not believe I was getting away with such dreadful material . . .'). It was decided to leave it all in his act, and his giggling helped turn him into a national institution.

He even managed to set the Queen off after a Royal Variety Performance. Standing in line along with the rest of the cast being introduced to Her Royal Highness, Tommy broke with protocol when it was his turn to have his hand shaken.

'I beg your pardon for my impertinence, Your Majesty,' said Tommy in his unmistakable voice. 'But do you like football?'

The Queen and her entourage looked suitably aghast. The rule is that you do not usually speak to Her Majesty until she has had the first word.

'If not,' Tommy continued, oblivious to the fact that he was trampling on forbidden territory, 'can I have your ticket for the FA Cup Final?'

Jennifer Saunders is arguably the great queen of the gigglers, and her wonderful creation *Absolutely Fabulous* often ran over time because the cast and crew were locked in unscripted laughter. When rehearsing for one episode, Jennifer performed some stretching exercises. As she bent forward she broke wind. Joanna Lumley, Julia Sawalha, Jane Horrocks and June Whitfield all fell about laughing.

Jennifer, who believed in writing and rewriting up to the shooting of each scene, realised it was gold-dust humour and added it to the script. It took several takes before they managed to do it because the sound-effects people could not quite get the farting volume right.

Jane Horrocks had to say the line immediately following it and kept corpsing to such an extent that her mascara started to run, and they had to call for make-up.

Yes, Absolutely Fabulous.

George C. Scott was not noted for his humour, but he had the entire cast and crew shaking with laughter when about to shoot a love scene with a particularly voluptuous actress. 'I apologise if I get an erection,' he said, as he got into bed alongside her. 'And I apologise if I don't.'

Burt Reynolds always prided himself on doing his own stunts across an acting career that straddled six decades. On the set of the 1998 film *Crazy Six*, the director told him he was bringing in a stuntman to take a fall.

'Over my dead body,' said an indignant Burt. 'I can still fall. Only problem I have is in getting up again!'

Cue collapse of director and crew.

Kenneth Branagh was playing Hamlet at Stratford-upon-Avon when, during a fight scene, his sword split in half. He began to giggle and then laugh wildly and as tears started to roll down his face he managed to turn it all into Hamlet having a fit.

'I started to laugh again after the show,' Branagh said, 'when a member of the audience told me she had never seen Hamlet played with such emotion!'

American chat show host Regis Philbin got a fit of the giggles in his news-reading days, and the director had to cut to a commercial. Unfortunately for Regis, his uncontrollable laughter had started just as he announced a newsflash that dozens of people had been killed in a train wreck in the Alps. 'Something from a previous news item had tickled me, and I started to smile,' he said. 'Then I really started to lose it as a piece of paper was stuffed into my hand announcing the train crash. I tried hard to control my face but I just broke up into helpless laughter. It was sheer torture.'

Comedian Stan Boardman, one of my Scouse buddies, once reduced a crew and audience to laughing wrecks. He was putting the case for Ian Rush to be rated a greater goalscorer than Jimmy Greaves in an ITV programme called *Who's the Greatest?* He called as one of his witnesses Liverpool and England goalkeeper Ray Clemence. All he had to say was, 'Ian Rush is a master with his feet . . . and now welcome somebody who handles balls better than anybody else . . .'

He just could not get the line out without corpsing, and had the studio in uproar. After twenty minutes of sheer bedlam – with Stan milking it for all his worth – he finally agreed to producer John D. Taylor's plea to change the introduction to: 'And now welcome Liverpool and England goalkeeper Ray Clemence.'

It was his funniest moment in a television studio since his 'Fokker'

Two Scouse scallies: Here I am with my Mersey pal Stan Boardman, who has still not forgiven the 'Jeer-mans' for bombing his chippie. He's a funny Fokker, that's for sure.

joke on *The Des O'Connor Show*, which made him too hot to handle for many television companies.

Stan can still set me off giggling just by saying: 'Don't like dem Jeermans. Dey bombed our chippie.'

I am reliably informed that Ricky Gervais is the current king of corpsers, who reduces just about everybody he works with to jelly. On the set of the ground-breaking series *The Office*, he was continually messing around off camera and making the cast and crew fall about. It made for a happy place to work, but sometimes a nightmare to get finished scenes into the can.

While most actors go into suppressed giggles trying to hold themselves together, Ricky has a disconcerting habit of laughing out loud like a hyena on heat. This wrecks any chance of the other actors recovering and carrying on as if nothing has happened.

The many out-takes from *The Office* are gold dust hunted by thousands of fans, and the majority of them are caused by Ricky's freewheeling humour. Amazingly, his daft disco dance – one of the most requested clips on television – was performed off the cuff and without a rehearsal. It took him thirty seconds, and then another thirty minutes to restore order among the watching cast and crew.

When Ricky and co-writer Stephen Merchant created their next masterpiece, *Extras*, they took the same casual, let's-have-a-laugh attitude on to the studio floor. In one scene Stephen (the agent) is drinking a cup of tea while telling Ricky about his next non-job. Every time he took a swig from the cup, Ricky tossed in an ad-lib that made Stephen choke and spit the tea out.

Ricky Gervais had a lot of good days at *The Office*, and put in extra effort in *Extras*. He delayed many scenes because of his continual corpsing. How about me getting together with him for a double act: The Two Rickys!

Nobody on *Extras* escaped the Gervais giggles.

Ross Kemp was supposed to be telling Ricky about his experiences as a tough-guy SAS officer, but was continually forced to walk off camera because of the faces Ricky was pulling . . . Kate Winslet, dressed as a nun, resorted to using the f-word to try to stop Ricky making her corpse . . . Samuel L. Jackson roared his way through a scene because Ricky kept losing it . . . Ben Stiller was supposed to be bollocking him in one scene and finished up with his arms around his neck crying with laughter . . . Les Dennis was brought to his knees laughing as Ricky reacted to seeing him bollock-naked in his dressing-room . . . Patrick Stewart had to sit through a dozen retakes as Ricky tried to respond to this great actor revealing how in a dream he had seen a beautiful girl losing her knickers.

If ever I have the pleasure of working with Ricky (*Ricky and Ricky, My Arse!*), I doubt if we would get a scene completed in a full day's shooting. It would be a battle of the gigglers, and not a dry eye in the house.

*Little Britain* duo Matt Lucas and David Walliams confess to being members of the corpsers' club, much of their giggling caused by their outrageous costumes. Walliams had one of his greatest laughs on set when he noticed that Lucas was playing an entire scene with his scrotum hanging loose for all to see. A floor manager eventually came and concealed the genitalia. Lucas couldn't do it himself because he was wearing long false fingernails. 'Spoilsport,' said Walliams to the floor manager after he had made the necessary adjustments.

Chris Barrie, man of a hundred voices, could not find one to break the unintended silence in a scene from *Red Dwarf* in which he played the haughty hologram Rimmer. He was supposed to light a cigar before delivering his line, but kept missing the end with his lighter. This led to laughter off camera which quickly spread to the audience, and continual corpsing before the scene could be finished. What made it so hilarious was that the show was famous for its technical wizardry, and here was its star unable to complete the simple task of lighting a cigar.

They were a happy crew on *Red Dwarf*, with lots of unplanned comedy mixed in and stirred with the superbly scripted stuff. Kryten (the robot brilliantly played by Robert Llewellyn) was responsible for a lot of the corpsing, often reducing Cat (Danny John-Jules) and Dave Lister (talented Scouser Craig Charles) to helpless laughter as he mangled his line and then went into reverse mode before starting it again.

And talking of reverse, there was one amazing *Red Dwarf* episode called 'Backwards' in which much of the dialogue was reversed. The subtitles put up on screen sometimes bore little relation to what was actually being said. For instance, when Lister berated Rimmer and Kryten for starting a fight, this – I am reliably informed by a *Red Dwarf* insider – is what he actually shouted: 'You are a stupid, square-headed, bald git, aren't you? Eh? I'm pointing at you, I'm pointing at you. But I'm not actually addressing you. I'm addressing the one prat in the country who's bothered to get hold of this recording, turn it round, and actually work out the rubbish that I'm saying. What a poor, sad life you've got! Bollocks to you!'

I wonder if there really was one person who managed to play the dialogue the right way round? He must have felt a right idiot when he heard what was being said. It would have made me corpse!

My good friend Sir John Mills told me this wonderful story of an entire cast that corpsed: 'An actor, playing a just-murdered corpse on stage in a whodunnit in a repertory performance in Birmingham, got an attack of the sneezes. It set off the five-actor cast into an explosion of giggles, and it continued for several minutes before the leading man, playing the detective, managed to ad-lib: "This heinous crime has caused great hysteria."'

*Seinfeld*, the series that set new comedic standards for sitcoms, was a hotbed of out-takes involving its four main characters, Jerry Seinfeld, Jason Alexander (George), Michael Richards (Kramer) and Julia Louis-Dreyfus (Elaine). There was a cracker when Kramer performed one of his aggressive entries into Jerry's apartment, flinging the door open in his unique style as I mentioned in Chapter 3. He went arse over tit into the kitchen area, but continued to try to deliver the line: 'Is my sweater back from the dry cleaners?' He was so dazed that it came out as, 'Is my sweater back from the dwy queeners?' It was twenty minutes before the laughter stopped.

*M\*A\*S\*H*, one of the longest-running comedies of all time, had hundreds of lines corpsed during its remarkable span of 251 episodes. The actors, including Alan Alda, were continually swearing as tongues twisted on lines, and there was a classic moment when McLean Stevenson (Lieutenant Colonel Henry Blake) was heard to shout, 'Gentlemen, gentlemen, please let's have less of this swearing . . . for f\*\*\*'s sake.'

No question that the wackiest of all modern corpsers is the versatile actor-comedian Robin Williams. From his earliest days in *Mork and Mindy*, he used to slip into a comedy routine the moment he cocked up a line and he would play to the audience with a volley of quick-fire jokes. One of his directors said: 'Robin turns corpsing into an advantage, and I have seen scriptwriters turn green as they have watched him produce far better material off the top of his head than anything that has been scripted for him. The man is a comic genius.'

The highest-paid corpsers were undoubtedly the six-strong ensemble of the American sitcom *Friends*, all of them notorious gigglers who used to bring scenes to a shrieking halt in front of the audience. They were each on $750,000 an episode. They giggled on set ... and then laughed all the way to the bank.

It was a cricket match that provided one of the funniest moments ever broadcast on radio, and one of the longest corpses to appear on a national station. During the England–West Indies Test match at The Oval in the summer of 1991, Ian Botham was dismissed in a freakish way when he clipped the top of the stumps with his boot when trying to avoid a ball. Jonathan Agnew, on *Test Match Special*, told the nation: 'Botham just couldn't quite get his leg over.'

His co-commentator Brian Johnston could be heard in the background trying to stifle a giggle. Then Aggers started to break up, saying: 'Oh stop it, Johnners.'

Johnston, who was one of the greatest of all the characters in the world of broadcasting, was then cued to give his summary of the day's play. All he could manage was to laugh uncontrollably into the microphone, with Agnew helpless alongside him.

It became – and continues to be – one of the most requested repeat moments in broadcasting history. The letters and phone calls started to flood in. Thousands of drivers had been listening in their cars on their way home and many had been forced to pull over to the side of the road until they had calmed down. Tim Rice said that he laughed so hard that he thought he was going to endanger his fellow motorists. Ronnie Corbett rang the BBC to say that his wife, Ann, who was at the wheel of their car, had to stop on the hard shoulder of the M1 while they both recovered.

There was a two-mile tailback at the entrance to the Dartford Tunnel on the M25 because some drivers were laughing so much they were unable to go through the tollbooths.

Listeners were literally reduced to tears. But there were those at the BBC who considered it unprofessional, and 'Aggers and Johnners' were kept apart for future broadcasts.

However, it was considered safe the following year to let them share the same *Test Match Special* microphone during a tea interval, taken up with answering listeners' letters.

As the umpires were coming out, Agnew selected one final letter from the pile and started to read it out. 'Can you please explain why in the game of cricket an appeals procedure is necessary or justifiable?' he began. 'This comes from . . .' He caught sight of the name and sniggered: 'Uh, from, uh . . . Berkshire.'

Aggers handed the letter quickly to Johnners, who tried to take over. 'It's not the Prime Minister William Pitt . . .' he chortled, suddenly spotting the name, '. . . but this is William H. *Titt* . . . and he says . . . he says . . .' It was too much for him. He collapsed in painful mirth, tears pouring down his face. Again, as a year earlier, the only sounds to be heard over the airwaves were wheezes and giggles. Fortunately, this time, summariser Trevor Bailey was at hand.

'The umpires are coming out,' he said, taking charge of the microphone. Brian was still unable to speak. 'Yes, here they are, Johnners,' Agnew said, getting his giggles under control. 'You move over. I'll do some commentary.'

As the game restarted, Johnners had to be helped, still weeping, from the box.

Laughter stopped play.

You will recall that when I started sharing this collection I described Peter Sellers as the Past President of the Gigglers' Club. Not the King. That title belonged to only one man: Terence Alan 'Spike' Milligan. 'Laughing was the only thing that kept me sane,' said this manic-depressive who managed to revolutionise comedy while battling with his inner demons.

*Beyond the Fringe*, *Monty Python*, *The Goodies*, *The Young Ones*, *Bottom*, *The Fast Show*, *The League of Gentlemen* and *Little Britain* all have to bow the knee to Spike as the father and founder of surreal, anarchic English humour. I was hooked from the first moment I heard him on radio in *The Goon Show* in the early 1950s. I remember the sketch well.

He went into a shop and said to the man behind the counter in his distinctive Eccles voice: 'Tell me, sir, do you know me?'

The man replied: 'No, I've never seen you before in my life.'

Eccles: 'Then how d'you know I'm me?'

It was nonsensical, but to this schoolboy with his ear pushed close to the crackly wireless in a two-up-and-two-down terraced house in Liverpool it was the gateway to a whole new world of humour that stretched the imagination while tickling the ribs.

For the next fifty years, between bouts of mental illness, Spike kept the world laughing. He could rarely complete a sketch without corpsing, and was often seen with tears running down his cheeks.

Right up into old age he was a very funny man. When told that *The Goons* had been released on CD, he said: 'I didn't know they were still in prison. And what's a CD? How d'you operate it? I still find the technology of a doorknob beyond me.'

Spike was the master of the ad-lib, and once had the whole of Australia screaming with laughter when interviewed live on air on the national broadcaster, the ABC. They made the mistake of letting Spike remain in the studio for the news broadcast that followed his interview. He constantly interjected his crazy interpretations of the news items to the point where the newsreader could hardly get a word out for laughing.

There was uproar, and the ABC executives ruled that Spike should never again be allowed to broadcast live on the station. Spike's reaction? 'In that case,' he said, 'I will in future do all my interviews with DEF.'

When his fellow Goon, rival giggler and close chum Harry Secombe was close to death's door, Spike told him: 'I'm so pleased you're going before me. I would hate to have you singing at my funeral.'

Spike brought the 1994 Comedy Awards to a screamingly hysterical standstill when a letter was read out from Prince Charles congratulating him on being honoured with a lifetime achievement award. Spike responded with: 'He's always been a grovelling little bastard.'

The next day he sent a fax to the Prince, saying: 'I suppose a knighthood is now out of the question?'

Prince Charles, a *Goon Show* fanatic who could impersonate all the characters, replied: 'I'm sorry, all the New Year's knighthoods are full up, but try a little light grovelling and one might come your way.'

Spike, who held an Irish passport, was awarded an honorary knighthood in 2000, two years before he passed on to the great comedy playhouse in the sky.

In accordance with his last wishes his headstone bears the Gaelic words, 'Dúirt mé leat go raibh mé breoite.'

Translated into English, these form the classic Milligan line, 'I told you I was ill.'

Yes, literally a corpsing line.

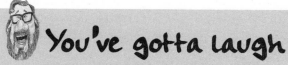 **You've gotta laugh**

Frank Sinatra is dining out at an exclusive Las Vegas restaurant one night when a New York businessman approaches him.

'Mr Sinatra,' he says, holding out a hand and fawning, 'I'm Marty Brightman from New York, your greatest fan, and I want to thank you for all the sheer joy you've given me over the years.'

'*My* pleasure,' says Sinatra, barely looking up from his spaghetti as he shakes Marty's hand.

'I'd like you to do me a big, big favour, Frank,' Marty says.

'What kinda favour?' asks the suddenly suspicious Sinatra.

'Well, I'm here with my, uh, secretary,' says Marty, giving a big wink. 'On your way outta the restaurant or when you go to the cloakroom I'd greatly appreciate it if you'd drop by my table and just take a second to say "Hi, Marty." It would make a great impression with my companion.'

'I'll do my best,' says Sinatra, who is in an unusually receptive mood. There was a time when he might have told Marty to go forth and multiply.

Twenty minutes later Sinatra prepares to leave, sees that Marty's table is on the way to the exit, and so decides to please his fan.

He walks up to the table and says, 'Hi, Marty. How's it going?'

Marty looks up and snaps, 'Don't bother me now, Frankie. Can't you see I've got company?'

## Hark who's talking nonsense

**HRH Prince Philip:**
'The grouse are in absolutely no danger from people who shoot grouse.'

**David Dimbleby:**
'. . . and there's the Victoria Memorial, built as a memorial to Victoria.'

**Brooke Shields:**
'Smoking kills. If you're killed you've lost a very important part of your life.'

**Elizabeth Taylor:**
'I haven't read any of the autobiographies about me.'

**John Humphrys:**
'And there's fog on the M25 in both directions.'

**Angela Rippon:**
'Not only is it the start of their honeymoon, it's the start of their married life together.'

**Rolf Harris:**
'And for those of you who don't know Australia House, it's a beautiful Victorian building . . . the first brick was laid in 1913 by King George V . . .'

**Richard Madeley:**
'And that's a self-portrait of himself, by himself.'

**Jeremy Paxman:**
'This parade marks the bicentenary of the storming of the Bastille some time ago. Two hundred years ago, in fact.'

**Nicholas Parsons:**
'Glenn Miller became a legend in his own lifetime due to his early death.'

**Edwina Currie:**
'There's no smoke without mud being flung around.'

**Julian Critchley:**
'That was not the only thing that he did. That was just the froth on the cake.'

**W. C. Fields:**
'I am free of all prejudices. I hate everyone equally.'

**Joan Rivers:**
'Boy George is all England needs – another queen who can't dress.'

**Dave Edison:**
'I'm desperately trying to figure out why kamikaze pilots wore helmets.'

**George Burns:**
'This is the sixth book I've written, which isn't bad for a guy who's only read two.'

**Spike Milligan:**
'A sure cure for seasickness is to sit under a tree.'

**Quentin Crisp:**
'The trouble with children is that they're not returnable.'

**Dick Cavett:**
'If your parents never had children, chances are you won't either.'

**Edgar Wallace:**
'An intellectual is someone who has found something more interesting than sex.'

**Michael Barrymore:**
'So Carol, you are a housewife and a mother. Do you have any children?'

**Samantha Fox:**
'I've got ten pairs of training shoes . . . one for each day of the week.'

**Nick Ross:**
'I wonder if we can speak through rose-tinted glasses?'

**Elaine Paige:**
'My shoe size is two and a half . . . the same size as my feet.'

**Bruce Forsyth:**
'Did you write the words for the song or the lyrics?'

**Steve Wright:**
'And don't forget that on Sunday you can hear the two-minute silence on Radio One.'

**Sir David Frost:**
'For those of you who have not read the book, it's being published tomorrow.'

# 6 Tales from the Dressing-room

Actors often spend more time in their dressing-rooms than on the set or stage. This is where the hottest gossip is exchanged and tales of the theatrical, movie and television worlds are passed on, and, more times than not, embellished beyond recognition by the time they come to their next telling.

I own up to loving a good old gossip, and the stories I share with you on the following pages have been carefully and gleefully garnered while sitting waiting for the call to 'action' on the next scene. I cannot guarantee their authenticity or accuracy, but I do know they will amuse you.

Sometimes I need to disguise the true identity of the leading players, as in the following true story that also features the peerless Eamonn Andrews. Those from my generation will tell you that Eamonn was one of the all-time great broadcasters, equally at home hosting *Sports Report*, presenting the original *What's My Line?* or tracking down celebrities with his famous Red Book and declaring, 'Tonight, *This Is Your Life.*'

However, Eamonn, for all his exposure and experience in nationwide television programmes, was as innocent as the day is long. He was a devout Roman Catholic who wrote a weekly column for the *Catholic Herald*, very rarely swore and led a pure life that would have earned the approval of a monk. He and the false glitter of show business were total strangers.

One of his searches for a star took him to Hollywood, where he surprised Dudley Moore with the Red Book. While in the green room waiting for the show to start, one of the most glamorous women in the world came in. She was to be a guest.

As Eamonn was introduced to her, she put a hand to her pretty forehead and said, 'God, I could do with some coke.'

'No problem,' said Eamonn, and off he scuttled to the bar – with the more worldly members of his *This Is Your Life* team wondering how he was going to satisfy her request.

Moments later, he returned with a glass of iced Coca-Cola and handed it to the beautiful creature.

'What on earth's this?' she snapped. 'I didn't mean this sort of coke.'

Eamonn, ever dutiful, returned to the bar and put in a new order. This time for a Pepsi.

He did not have a sniff of an idea what the lady had meant.

Another Eamonn story. He was the host of a huge, televised party to celebrate the three hundredth edition of the ITV version of *This Is Your Life* (he had also presented the BBC show for fourteen years before the switch to commercial television). Nearly all of the three hundred guests who had been honoured were there, including king of the hellraisers Oliver Reed.

He was seated at a table for twelve directly opposite *Emmerdale* actor Patrick Mower. They did not know each other. As the evening progressed and Reed got more and more pissed he took an unnatural and growing dislike to Mower. 'His drunken gaze was burning right through me,' Patrick was to say later.

Suddenly Reed got unsteadily to his feet, staggered around the table and confronted Mower, who stood up as if ready to give him a friendly greeting. Reed ignored his proffered handshake and butted him right between the eyes.

Eamonn saw what had happened, and while guests screamed and *This Is Your Life* staff wondered how to handle Reed – an out-of-control drunken bull of a man – he had the good sense to ask another guest to sort it out.

The man Eamonn picked out was Fred 'Nosher' Powell, who had been a good-class professional heavyweight boxer and had gone on to become one of Britain's leading stuntmen. Nosher got Reed in an arm-lock, led him out of the plush dining-room and poured him into a taxi.

Eamonn said to Nosher later, 'Sorry to have forced you into a comeback.'

Cockney Fred said: 'Just as well you picked me to sort it out rather than the geezer sitting next to me.'

Nosher had been sitting alongside former Prime Minister Edward Heath.

I could fill the book with Oliver Reed stories, most of them associated with booze and brawling. But I will settle for one more that director Ken Russell tells about the famous nude wrestling scene between Reed and Alan Bates in *Women in Love*.

'Oliver was immensely proud of his manhood,' said Russell. 'In fact his favourite party trick was to show off the clawed bird that he'd had tattooed on it one drunken night. When it came to the wrestling scene, he quietly prepared for it by disappearing behind a curtain. You had to hand it to him, he was very competitive and was not going to allow himself to look small alongside Bates. Both of them came out of it with their pride intact!'

I'll kick off the following scatter-gun collection of stories with another anecdote from *This Is Your Life* . . .

Serial bride Zsa Zsa Gabor was the star presented with the Red Book by Eamonn Andrews in Los Angeles the week after he had caught out Dudley Moore. The carefully planned surprise conclusion to the show involved bringing on the prize stallion that Zsa Zsa loved above anything else. The feeling, apparently, was mutual. The *This Is Your Life* production team were told that the stallion got very aroused just at the scent of his owner. All eyes were on the undercarriage when the horse was announced, and as the stallion approached Zsa Zsa there were gasps of amazement as he gave what can only be described as a big ending to the show.

When I was plastering for a living a favourite pin-up of my workmates was a curvy sex-bomb of a platinum blonde called Diana Dors. She was known as Britain's answer to Marilyn Monroe. One day at the height of her fame she returned to her home town of Swindon to open a church fête.

While lunching with the vicar before the opening ceremony she let slip that her real name was Diana Fluck. This name managed to burn itself into the vicar's brain, and he kept trying to push it away because he had to introduce her and did not want to make a silly error.

At last it was time to open the fête, and the vicar uttered the immortal words: 'Ladies and gentlemen, it is with great pleasure that I introduce our star guest . . . we all love her and especially as she is our local girl. I therefore feel it right to introduce her by the name many of you here know her by . . . ladies and gentlemen, Miss Diana Clunt.'

There are dozens of Tommy Cooper stories that continue to do the rounds long after the king of funny men went to the great dressing-room in the sky. Here are five of my favourites:

- Tommy got out of a taxi one day and slipped what seemed to be a folded fiver into the driver's breast pocket. 'Have a drink on me, pal,' said Tommy with a smile and a wink. The driver later discovered that Tommy had generously tipped him with a teabag.

- Advised to go on a diet because of his huge bulk, big drinker Tommy elected to make it a whisky diet. He later reported: 'It's working. I've lost three days already.'

- Tommy was a useful heavyweight boxer when serving in the Welsh Guards. During one fight he took a lot of punishment. Later he reported: 'As I went back to my corner the second told me: "You're boxing well, son. He's not laying a glove on you."

- 'I replied: "Well keep an eye on the flipping ref. Somebody's whacking me."'

- A Cooper classic: 'I went to the butcher's the other day and bet him fifty quid that he couldn't reach the meat on his top shelf. He refused to take the bet. Said the steaks were too high.'

- And another from the great man: 'Went to the doctor last week because I had a cucumber stuck in one ear, a carrot in the other and two peas up my nose. "What's the matter with me, doc?" I asked.

- 'He told me: "You're not eating properly."'

'A funny thing happened to me on the way to the publishers . . .' I have always fancied myself as a stand-up comedian and have done quite a lot of club work. My fellow Scouser Tom O'Connor (left) and gifted Welsh actor Philip Madoc (right) seem to be enjoying my little act. Tom recently celebrated his 65th birthday, and so he is now nearly as old as my jokes.

Morecambe and Wise, arguably the greatest British double act of them all, used to make weekly flights to and from the United States to appear on the prestigious, coast-to-coast *Ed Sullivan Show*. 'The first time we were introduced by Ed,' recalled Eric, 'the viewers at home were convinced we were a trio. His introduction went like this: "And now, from Britain, please welcome the funniest guys you'll ever meet. More . . . Cambe and Wise." Viewers kept expecting the third man to walk in on our act at any time.'

Fancy walking into a theatre and finding Tommy Cooper and Morecambe and Wise on the same bill! It happened in Torquay during a summer season at the Princess Theatre before the three of them had become the most popular funny men in the land.

'We talked Tommy into doing the "death valley" opening spot throughout the season,' Eric said. 'Ernie and I would then find places to hide from where we could quietly heckle him by just saying "tut tut" as if disapproving of his material.

'Tommy used to spend half his act trying to work out where we were. Sometimes we were in the wings, or up in the flies. At poorly attended shows we would sit in the audience, and another time we made Tommy crack up by sitting in with the orchestra holding saxophones. He always got his own back simply by putting on an act that was impossible to follow. And who followed him? We did!'

'Tut tut' is a very gentle heckle compared with what some comedians had to face, particularly on the old working men's clubs circuit where you took your life in your hands with some of the beer-stoked audiences. Bernard Manning tells of the best heckle he ever heard, and it's a story told against himself:

'One of the punters at my Manchester club left his table while I was in full flow. I got them to put the spotlight on him, and I said: "How would you like it if I walked out on you while you were performing?" He brought the house down with the comeback: "Sorry, mate, I was just going for a quick piss before the comedian comes on."'

But my advice is don't mess with Manning! He has one of the

most potent tongues in show business, and he takes no prisoners. If you heckle him you are likely to be put down with a snorter like: 'If I wanted to hear from an arsehole I would have farted.'

If you are going to heckle, just remember that the comedian has the microphone. I asked some of my comedian pals their favourite put-downs for hecklers . . .


Stan Boardman: 'If shit was music, pal, you'd be an orchestra.'

Ken Dodd (studying his watch): 'I think it's time for your medication.'

Frank Carson: 'I see that a village is short of its idiot tonight.'

Faith Brown: 'Save your breath . . . you'll need it to blow up your date later.'

Norman Collier: 'Ah, I recognise you. Your father was a boxer (pause) and your mother a Dalmatian. (pause) You've inherited your mum's spots.'

This is a response attributed to the rotund old comedian Fred Emney Jr when a woman autograph hunter asked how he got so fat: 'Because, my dear, every time I f***ed your mother she gave me a biscuit.'

The lugubrious Les Dawson had a great line to shut up hecklers: 'This is what happens when cousins marry.'

Jasper Carrott would keep them quiet with lines like: 'Why don't you talk to the wall . . . that's plastered as well.'

Julian Clary has a whole range of vicious put-downs. They include: 'Men like you don't grow on trees . . . they swing from them.'

Then there's the silencer from Les Dennis: 'Excuse me! Do I come to your work and tell you how to use your broom?'

Bob Monkhouse was a genius at thinking on his feet. Once, when his stand-up act was interrupted by a noisy heckler, he ad-libbed: 'Does matron know you're out?'

A cracker passed down the generations features the great tragedian Barry Sullivan, who was performing in *Richard III* in Glasgow. When he came to the scene in which, after the battle, Richard cries, 'A horse! A horse! My kingdom for a horse,' a voice from the balcony cried, 'Will an ass do?'

'Yes,' Sullivan replied, 'come down at once!'

And we stay in Glasgow for perhaps the most vicious put-down of them all. It comes from the Big Yin, Billy Connolly: 'When God put teeth in that mouth he wasted a perfectly good arsehole.'

Few would disagree that the modern king of one-liners is multi-talented comedian, actor, director and jazz clarinettist Woody Allen. Here's the maestro on matters of life and death:

- 'I don't want to achieve immortality through my work . . . I want to achieve it through not dying.'
- 'It is impossible to experience one's death objectively and still carry a tune.'
- 'On the plus side, death is one of the few things that can be done just as easily lying down.'
- 'There are worse things in life than death. Have you ever spent an evening with an insurance salesman?'
- 'How can I believe in God when just last week I got my tongue caught in the roller of an electric typewriter?'
- 'If it turns out that there is a God, I don't think that He's evil. But the best that you can say about Him is that basically He's an underachiever.'
- 'If only God would give me some clear sign! Like making a large deposit in my name in a Swiss bank.'
- 'To you I'm an atheist; to God, I'm the Loyal Opposition.'
- 'Life is divided into the horrible and the miserable.'
- 'Life is full of misery, loneliness and suffering – and it's all over much too soon.'
- 'I tended to place my wife under a pedestal.'
- 'Money is better than poverty, if only for financial reasons.'
- 'Eighty per cent of success is showing up.'

There is an English-born comedian who was in the Woody Allen class for one-liners. Any guesses? I am talking about Bob Hope, who emigrated to the States from Eltham in Kent and became one of the most popular (and richest) comedians in the history of show business. 'I left England at the age of four,' he said, 'when I discovered there was no chance that I could become King.'

There was a major difference between Hope and Allen (sounds a good title for a double act). Hope employed a team of gag-writers, while Allen's work is largely his own creation.

Bob Monkhouse (who was as good as any British comedian at delivering quick-fire jokes) went to the States to work as one of Hope's scriptwriters. 'We churned out jokes as if we were working in a sausage factory,' he said. 'Bob was a master at delivering them, but you always thought that it was your baby and that he was taking the credit for having given birth.'

Heckled in a good-natured way when making a speech at a fund-raising event, Hope ad-libbed: 'You wouldn't heckle if I had my writers with me!'

He liked to be topical, and often had politicians in his sights. When John F. Kennedy started his run to the White House, Hope said: 'This is a triumph for democracy. It just goes to show that a millionaire has as good a chance as anybody else.'

He was notorious for carefully hoarding his money ('He has a Bob Hope suite at Fort Knox,' cracked his screen partner Bing Crosby). But this didn't stop Hope bashing the banks with his jokes. 'A bank', he said, 'is a place that will lend you money if you can prove you don't need it.'

Few, if any, comedians have travelled as much as Hope. As well as his globetrotting *Road* films with Crosby, he regularly entertained US troops posted overseas, and played golf on every continent. He came up with the line: 'I've been almost as many places as my luggage.'

The best comedians in the land would not have wanted to cross swords with Winston Churchill. These were some of his great off-the-cuff remarks:

- Nancy Astor: 'You're drunk.'
- Churchill: 'And you're ugly. But in the morning, I shall be sober.'
- Nancy Astor: 'If you were my husband, I would poison your coffee.'
- Churchill: 'Madam, if you were my wife, I'd drink it.'
- (of Charles de Gaulle): 'What can you do with a man who looks like a female llama surprised while bathing?'
- (when, in his veteran years, told his flies were undone at a dinner table): 'No matter. The dead bird does not leave the nest.'
- (of Clement Attlee): 'A modest man who has a good deal to be modest about.'
- (of Viscount Montgomery): 'In defeat unbeatable; in victory unbearable.'
- (in a debate on the poor usage of English grammar): 'This is the sort of English up with which I will not put.'

However, the king of the put-down line was without doubt the legendary Groucho Marx. Here is just a sample:

- 'I never forget a face, but in your case I'll make an exception.'
- (responding to a clergyman who had thanked him for all the enjoyment he'd given to the world): 'And I want to thank you for all the joy you've taken out of it.'
- (taking a pulse in the film *A Day at the Races*): 'Either this man is dead, or my watch has stopped.'
- 'From the moment I picked up the book I was convulsed with laughter. One day I intend to read it.'
- 'I do beg your pardon ma'am . . . I thought you were a guy I knew in Pittsburgh.'

- (asked if Groucho was his real name): 'No, I'm breaking it in for a friend.'
- (when refused permission to join a Californian leisure club because he was Jewish): 'As my daughter is only half Jewish, would it be possible for her to go into your pool just up to her knees?'
- (on being offered membership of a country club): 'I would not want to belong to a club that would have somebody like me as a member.'

Dorothy Parker, perhaps the only other person in Groucho's class for acerbic put-downs, made a point that many comedians and scriptwriters will understand. 'Writing humour is the hardest thing,' she said, 'because everybody and anybody has the right to read it and say, "I don't think that's funny."'

It was Dorothy, a renowned screenwriter and gossip columnist, who came up with the following witty lines:

- 'You can lead a horticulture, but you cannot make her think.'
- (on being told that the infamously quiet President Calvin Coolidge had died): 'How could they tell?'
- (after a publisher left a message with her secretary that he was still waiting for her manuscript): 'Tell him I'm f***ing busy, or vice versa.'
- 'This is not a novel to be tossed aside lightly. It should be thrown with great force.'
- (writing about a first-night performance by Katharine Hepburn): 'She ran the whole gamut of the emotions from A to B.'
- 'One more drink and I'd have been under the host.'
- 'The only "ism" in Hollywood is plagiarism.'
- 'Scratch a lover, and find underneath a foe.'

- 'Men seldom make passes at girls who wear glasses.'
- (after an abortion): 'It serves me right for putting all my eggs in one bastard.'

If I had to pick somebody from this side of the Atlantic to put up against the likes of Groucho Marx and Dorothy Parker, I would select Spike Milligan. Here are just a few of his sayings:

- 'I thought I'd begin by reading a poem by Shakespeare, but then I thought, why should I? He never reads any of mine.'
- 'I'm Irish. We think sideways.'
- (on receiving an honorary CBE in 1992): 'I can't see the sense in it really. It makes me a Commander of the British Empire. They might as well make me a Commander of Milton Keynes – at least that exists!'
- 'And God said, "Let there be light" and there was light, but the Electricity Board said he would have to wait until Thursday to be connected.'
- (on whether he wanted to go to heaven): 'I'd like to go there. But if bloody Jeffrey Archer is there I want to go to Lewisham.'
- 'Contraceptives should be used on every conceivable occasion.'
- 'Is there anything worn under the kilt? No, it's all in perfect working order.'
- 'Chopsticks are one of the reasons the Chinese never invented custard.'
- 'How long was I in the army? Five foot eleven. I was equally as long in *The Goons*.'
- 'I don't mind dying. I just don't want to be there when it happens.'

Spike Milligan's *Goon Show* laughter-mate Peter Sellers told this true story that you could not make up:

'I received this letter from a *Goon Show* fan . . .

'"Dear Mr Sellers,

'"I have been a keen follower of yours on *The Goon Show*, and should be most grateful if you would kindly send me a singed [*sic*] photograph of yourself . . ."

'I showed it to Harry Secombe who agreed with me on the only course of action. Very carefully I burned the edges of one of my publicity photographs with my cigarette lighter – and, with much giggling, sent it off by return mail . . .

'A week or so later, another letter arrived from the same fan:

'"Dear Mr Sellers,

'"Thank you very much for the photograph, but I wonder if I could trouble you for another as this one is signed all round the edge . . ."'

When growing up in Swansea in the 1930s, Harry Secombe came under the wing of an English teacher who was impressed by his creative writing and encouraged him to set his sights on becoming a journalist. Harry left school with every intention of fulfilling his teacher's dream. But the war intervened, and Harry joined the army. By the time he was demobbed in 1945 he had changed his target from journalist to entertainer.

Years later the now famous Sir Harry returned to Swansea in his Rolls-Royce and decided to pay his old teacher a visit. He parked outside the teacher's tiny terraced house, knocked on the door, and moments later pupil and teacher were regarding each other for the first time in decades. 'My dear Harry boy,' said the old man, shaking his head sadly, 'what went wrong?'

When American comedian Joe E. Lewis saw Billy Wilder's searing film adaptation of *The Lost Weekend* – about the horrors of alcoholism – he said: 'That's it, I'm giving up ... I have sworn off ... I am through ... (Pause) ... I will never go to see another picture again!'

Stan Boardman tells this cracker which will strike a chord with anybody who has ever had a third-rate agent: 'When I first came into the business I was advised to get a press agent, somebody who could put it about that there was a new kid on the block. So I hired one at fifty quid a week, which was a lot of money in those days. The first week, no press at all. I called my agent and asked: "What's happening?" He said, "They're talking about you, Stan, they're talking about you."

This is me with Sir Norman Wisdom, the funniest of funny men when I was a youngster. What was considered hilarious then would be classed as corny now, but he had the nation in stitches. Sir Norman was up there with the likes of Eric Morecambe, Tommy Cooper and Ken Dodd as one of the king clowns of the 20th century.

'Two more weeks go by, another hundred pounds, and no press. I'm pretty pissed off. I called my agent and said, "Hey, what's going on? I'm not even mentioned in the births, deaths and marriages." He said, "They're talking about you, Stan, they're talking about you."

'Five weeks later, still not a single mention. All that money down the drain and nothing to show for it. I decided to go to the agent's office to find out what he was doing for me. "What's happening?" I asked. "What've I got to show for my two hundred and fifty quid?"

'"They're talking about you, Stan, they're talking about you," he said, like a broken record.

'I said, "Oh yeah? So what are they saying?"

'He replied, "They're saying, 'Whatever happened to Stan Boardman?'"'

You will soon realise who told me the following story:

One day a doctor was visited by a patient complaining of depression. After examining him, the doctor said: 'There's nothing wrong with you medically. You just need cheering up. Go and see Ken Dodd's show. He will make you laugh, and will be better for you than any drugs.'

'Thank you, Doctor,' the patient said, 'but I am Ken Dodd!'

That creative entertainer Victor Borge had a saying that was a beautiful summary of why comedy is such a magnet: 'A smile is the shortest distance between two people.' The great Dane did not just make audiences smile, he made them roar with laughter. He was a trained concert pianist (playing a piano made by Steinway & Sons, he would say: 'I did not even know Steinway was married . . !'), and cleverly mixed his skill at the keyboard with a wit that was C sharp.

He was once playing an old piano with yellowing keys during one of his concerts. When somebody asked why the keys had yellowed, he said: 'The elephant smoked too much.'

Borge wanted something to occupy him away from the concert hall and came up with the idea of running a chicken farm. 'But do you know anything about breeding chickens?' he was asked. 'No,' he said, 'but the chickens do.'

In his later years, he announced: 'Today, my friends, I am celebrating my seventy-fifth birthday, which is rather embarrassing because I am eighty-five.'

Liberace was another entertainer who was a trained concert pianist. He took showmanship to a new level that earned him ridicule from the classical world, but an army of fans – mostly middle-aged women – across the globe. I loved the opening line he often used. Waving fingers loaded with huge diamond rings, he would tell his audience: 'Take a good look. You're entitled to. After all, you paid for them.'

Responding to the critics who used to hammer his showing-off style of piano playing (he once hit six thousand distinct notes in two minutes), Liberace said: 'These people don't realise how much they hurt me. They make me cry all the way to the bank.'

Jack Benny played up to his reputation as the stingiest comedian in the world. Once he was held up in the street by a mugger with a gun. 'Your money or your life,' the mugger said. Benny did not reply. 'You deaf, fellah?' said the mugger. 'Your money or your life?' At last Benny replied: 'I'm weighing it up . . . I'm weighing it up.'

Johnny Vegas, who is more on the edge with his comedy than a tightrope walker without a safety net, started out in a club where he agreed to do his act just for free beer. After a couple of nights the management counted the empty bottles and told him: 'In future, we'll pay you.'

I shot a film with Johnny called *The Virgin of Liverpool*. He was hilarious company, and told me how he could not walk down the street without somebody shouting, 'Where's your monkey?' This was a reference to the woollen monkey he appeared with in a series of TV adverts.

'Finally,' said Johnny, 'I cracked, and when one person too many shouted "Where's your monkey?" I shouted back, "It f***ing died!"'

Pure Vegas.

While working on one of his early films – *Play It Cool* – director Michael Winner was prone to pass on his directions to the cast at close quarters through a megaphone. An irritated cast member decided to stop this and put sneezing powder on the end of the megaphone. After a sneezing fit, such close-up commands stopped. It was years later before the culprit owned up on Winner's *This Is Your Life* tribute show. Take a bow Lionel Blair.

Winner was excited about working with Joan Collins on his remake of *The Big Sleep*. But Joan was not keen on getting up early for hair and make-up, and declared that she wanted to wear a wig for the film.

Despite Winner insisting that she went natural, Joan secretly wore a wig that was put on and fixed to her head with dozens of pins. The wig looked so real that Winner accepted that it was her real hair . . . after trying – and failing – to pull it off, with Joan feigning that he was pulling her hair out.

At the end of the shoot, Joan announced that she had a surprise for Winner . . . and she pulled off her wig and threw it at him.

These days the director turned fierce restaurant critic would complain very loudly about a stray hair . . . especially in his soup.

David 'Mr Cool' Niven did not leg it to Hollywood when World War Two broke out. He did his duty and joined the army. He recalled on a television chat show: 'We were building up for the big counter-attack against Hitler, and my battalion was involved in one of those tedious military exercises carried out as rehearsals for the real thing. On this occasion, the general commanding our side thought it would be a good idea to try out the merits of homing pigeons as message carriers and rather rashly selected me for the task.

'Accordingly I found myself ensconced comfortably enough in a pub well behind the make-believe "enemy" lines, from which I was supposed to send back information about troop movements. However, as the hours slipped past, nothing whatever happened, and the pigeons cooed away happily in their baskets. Finally, feeling I had to justify the exercise in some way, I encoded a message, attached it to a bird's leg, and released it, little thinking it would ever get into the right hands.

'To my amazement, the bird duly arrived where and when it was supposed to and everyone, including the general, clustered round the signals officer while he decoded the message. Rather flippantly, I had written: "I have been sent home for pissing in my basket." Bang went that weekend's leave.'

You will need to be of a certain age to have heard of a comedian called Arthur Askey, a Scouser who moved to London and became one of the giants of radio and early television. Mind you, he was not a physical giant and had to stand on his toes to make five foot five. His 'before your very eyes' catchphrase was known in every household.

Following the glorious escape of our troops from Dunkirk in 1940, Arthur took some of his showbiz pals along to a Liverpool army hospital and spent three hours entertaining the troops in their wards. As he was about to leave, the matron called him to one side and thanked him for putting on a show for the lads.

'It's the least we could do after what they went through on the beaches at Dunkirk,' said Arthur.

'The beaches of Dunkirk?' said the matron. 'None of this lot has been farther than Blackpool beach. This is a VD hospital.'

George Burns was an exceptionally funny man, and he had an incredibly long career in which to learn his trade. Even in his nineties he was still cracking storming jokes: 'I was out walking in the park this morning when I saw a beautiful girl pass by. I turned as quickly as my walking frame would allow to see the rear department, and that was as good as the front. "Oh," I thought, "to be seventy again!"'

Another great gag from Burns, and this long after his wonderful wife Gracie Allen had passed on: 'My current girlfriend told me about a book I could get from the library that would help me find her G-spot. I searched high and low and couldn't find the book.'

The *Burns and Allen* show was one of the first big comedy imports to hit British television screens from the United States. We had been fed on a diet of 'I say, I say, I say' variety entertainment, and it was a real eye (and ear) opener to see how funny sitcom humour could be. The show ran from 1950 to 1958, and made Burns and Allen world famous after they had worked together for thirty years as a vaudeville double act and then on radio. One of the surprises was how funny Gracie Allen was. Women at that time found it very difficult to be accepted as (and I hope this makes sense) seriously funny in the UK.

To give you an idea of how witty Gracie was, George Burns — one of the funniest people ever to crack a joke — was reduced to the straight man.

The format of the show was simple enough. It was set in the Burns' home, with George cast in the dual role of on-screen narrator of their life together and foil for Gracie and her gloriously scatterbrained adventures. George was unflappable. He would simply turn to the camera, trademark cigar in hand, and philosophise to the audience on life with Gracie.

George summed it all up beautifully when he said: 'To be a straight man you have to have a talent. You have to develop this talent, then you gotta marry her, like I did.'

Following the death of his beloved Gracie in 1964, George started a new career as a solo artist and developed into a fine actor. Neil Simon's *The Sunshine Boys*, in which he co-starred with Walter Matthau, is as funny and as poignant a film about the world of the comedian as you will ever see.

George earned an Oscar for his performance. I think it should have been a joint award, because Walter Matthau – as his grumpy double-act partner – was his equal. Receiving his Oscar, eighty-year-old Burns said: 'It couldn't have happened to an older guy. I have discovered the secret of being a successful movie actor, and I am happy to share it with you. Make one film every thirty-six years. Can't wait for the next one.'

I found another side to George Burns while watching a TV chat show on which he reminisced about life after Gracie. He said that he whiled away the time on the golf course, even though he detested the game. 'Mark Twain knew what he was talking about when he called it a good walk spoiled,' he said. 'I even lose my ball in the ball wash.'

His regular partner was the comic genius Harpo Marx, who spent his entire career convincing audiences that he was a mute while in reality he was an intellectual who mixed (and conversed) with America's leading philosophers and politicians.

'Harpo took his golf with deadly seriousness,' said Burns. 'He regularly shot the low eighties, while I was hacking around near the hundred mark. But I told him that I got better value for my money because I saw the entire course, not just the fairway. It drove Harpo nuts when I used to sing while addressing the ball.

'There was one particular game when Harpo was having the round of his life. We came to the final eighteenth hole, a monster par five, and Harpo knew that if he could get down in par he would get under eighty for the first time ever.

'The green on this eighteenth was elevated and surrounded by sand traps. I winced as Harpo's third shot landed in one of the traps. Suddenly he was under pressure for his par.

'Because I didn't want to disturb Harpo or make him nervous, I stayed at the bottom of the hill while he climbed to the top and got ready to take his crucial bunker shot.

'Suddenly he looked down at me standing at the bottom of the hill and said, "What are you doing down there, George?"

'I called back, "You're close to breaking eighty. I don't want to upset you by watching you hit out of the trap." And he said, "You're upsetting my concentration. Come on up here, like you always do."

'So I told him OK and I trudged up the hill and stood on the edge of the trap while he was preparing to strike the ball. I looked the other way so I wouldn't upset him.

'But then he asked, "Why aren't you watching me, George, like you always do?" And I explained again, "Harpo, I don't want to upset you." And again he said, "You *are* upsetting me. Act naturally. Do exactly what you always do."

'So just as he took his backswing, I started to sing "When Irish Eyes Are Smiling" in a very loud voice. He missed the ball completely, and triple bogeyed the hole.

'He gave me the famous Harpo silent treatment for the rest of the day, but we stayed friends . . . and I kept on singing on the course.'

Dennis Christopher was appearing opposite Farrah Fawcett in *Butterflies Are Free* at the Burt Reynolds Dinner Theatre in Jupiter, Florida. Suddenly, during the opening-night performance, a mentally disturbed woman in the front row started yelling insults and making bird calls before suddenly raising her dress and flashing the performers. Christopher was so astonished and shocked that he put his hands over his face. The character he was playing was supposed to be blind!

A friend of mine spends his time creating funny anagrams from celebrity names. Here are some clever examples:

> GEORGE BUSH . . .
> HE BUGS GORE

> TONY BLAIR PM . . .
> BAN LIMP TORY

> PRESIDENT CLINTON OF THE USA . . .
> *TO COPULATE HE FINDS INTERNS*

> And he came up with RAIN MISTS MY ROYLE CONK from
> RICKY TOMLINSON MY ARSE

> Here's one from me . . .
> FIT EAGLE
> GET A LIFE

When Hugh Grant was auditioning for the lead role in *Four Weddings and a Funeral* he took along a tape of a speech he had made as best man at his brother's wedding. It helped him clinch the part. He recalled: 'I am quite proud of the speech I made because it did turn out to be quite funny. Luckily my brother got a very bad sty in his eye on the day of his wedding and he begged me not to talk about it. So I got up and said, "I'm not going to mention my brother's sty, even though it's the biggest sty I have ever seen in my life or in medical history." And I went on and on, all about his sty, things like, "I hope that his wife will keep him in the sty to which he has become accustomed", and 'My sty and I . . ." It seemed to go down well. That's why I showed it to the *Four Weddings* producers, and they said that was just the sort of thing they had in mind.'

A few weeks after the release of *Die Another Day*, which also starred the beautiful Halle Berry, Pierce Brosnan was walking through Dublin's Phoenix Park, when a young man spotted him. The fan asked to shake his hand. Brosnan complied, and a huge smile came over the youngster's face. Holding up his own hand, the Dubliner exclaimed with satisfaction, 'That's the closest I will ever come to having my hand on Halle Berry's arse!'

Radio Five Live football favourite Stuart Hall – for years the giggling voice of *It's a Knockout* – came home late after a liquid celebration party. He slipped into bed next to his wife only to wake her moments later complaining that he was paralysed and could not move his legs at all. 'The diagnosis was instant,' Hall later recalled, with that trademark laugh. 'My wife peeled back the bedclothes and revealed that I had simply put both my legs in one pyjama trouser leg.'

Shaun Williamson is famed as Barry in *EastEnders* and immortalised by Ricky Gervais and Stephen Merchant in *Extras* as 'Fat Barry'. But the hapless Barry was not his first role in the soap. A few months before his arrival in Albert Square, Shaun was cast as a paramedic. He won a role with two lines . . . that of Paramedic 1.

The thing is, Paramedic 1 needed to be able to drive as he was behind the wheel of the ambulance. Shaun revealed that he could not drive and so was given the part of Paramedic 2 . . . with ten times the dialogue.

The problem of not being able to drive cropped up again when Shaun was playing Barry, whom the producers decided should be a car salesman. Every time his character had to pull away in a car, Shaun would get out of the motor and make way for a look-alike.

'It was becoming embarrassing,' said Shaun, 'so I quietly booked myself some driving lessons and passed first time. Not sure my body double was that pleased, though!'

I've heard the following golden oldie dozens of times, but Max Bygraves claims it as his original: 'I am always being asked to visit old folks' homes. Not long ago I went to one and was wandering around meeting the staff and residents when I came across one old girl who seemed keen to talk.

'"D'you know who I am?" I asked her.

'"No," she replied. "But ask matron, she'll tell you."'

Les Dawson was one of the cleverest comedians of modern times, playing with words and painting pictures in the imagination of his listeners that made the jokes twice as funny. Although they upset the PC brigade, I loved his mother-in-law jokes, particularly this one: 'The wife's mother told me, "When you're dead, I'll dance on your grave." I said, "Good, I'm being buried at sea!"'

He showed his ma-in-law no mercy. Another of his classics: 'The wife's mother has been married three times. Her first two died through eating poisoned mushrooms. The third one died with an arrow in his back. I said to her: "How terrible! How come he was killed by an arrow?"

'She said: "Because he wouldn't eat the bloody mushrooms."'

They don't make 'em like Les Dawson any more. The bloody PC mob broke the mould.

Music has always played an important part in my life. I grew up in a Liverpool that was a hotbed of revolutionary sounds that changed the face (or should that be the ears?) of pop music for ever. There were The Beatles, of course, but the Fab Four were just the talented tip of an iceberg, with Gerry and the Pacemakers, Rory Storm and the Hurricanes (featuring a young Ringo Starr on drums) and dozens of other groups all adding to the new Mersey beat. There was also Hobo Rick and the Hi-Fi Three. That was the group I formed with three buddies, with me showing off on the banjo and singing skiffle-style songs.

I still strum the old banjo today, and recorded a CD of my favourite songs called *Music My Arse*. Some said I had a bare-faced cheek. It was not so much released as escaped, and the last I heard it had entered the charts in Outer Mongolia, where they play it to frighten away the wolves.

The main track was a cover of 'Are You Looking At Me', and I got to sing it on *Parkinson* with Noddy Holder, Geoffrey Hughes and my old *Brookside* buddy Michael Starke helping me belt it out. Noddy is a man who strikes a hard bargain, and he held out for twelve bacon sarnies and a free week's kip in my caravan as his fee for recording with me.

He could talk for England, and is great company. He had me falling about with the following story, told in his heavy Midlands accent:

'I was in a retro clothes shop trying on a pair of gold lamé trousers, and was admiring them in the mirror when the assistant asked if I'd like to try on a silver shirt too, which I did. I looked fantastic. Then the assistant said: "Would sir like a kipper tie?" I replied, "Not 'alf, I'm parched. Milk and two sugars, please."'

I'd better give a translation for those not used to Brum-speak. 'Kipper tie' in a Midlands accent becomes 'cuppa tea'. Geddit?

My Scouse pal Les Dennis, who has developed from comedian to a super all-round actor, will always be associated with *Family Fortunes*, a show he presented for an astonishing run of sixteen years. I asked him what was the funniest answer he ever got during the Money Game round. He told me: 'The question was "Name a popular TV soap." The woman contestant answered: "Dove!"'

Les came to my wedding when I married Rita, and we pinned him down to naming the Top Twenty daftest answers on *Family Fortunes*. His survey said . . .

Q. Name a song with 'moon' in the title
A. *Blue Suede Moon*

Q. Name a bird with a long neck
A. *Naomi Campbell*

Q. Name an occupation where you need a torch
A. *A burglar*

Q. Name a famous brother and sister
A. *Bonnie and Clyde*

Q. Name a dangerous race
A. *The Arabs*

Q. Name something that floats in the bath
A. *Water*

Q. Name something you wear on the beach
A. *A deckchair*

Q. Name a type of horse
A. *Clothes*

Q. Name a famous royal
A. *Mail*

Q. Name a number you have to memorise
A. *7*

Q. Name something in the garden that's green
A. *House*

Q. Name a famous bridge
A. *The bridge over troubled water*

Q. Name something associated with the police

A.  *Pigs*

Q.  Name a sign of the zodiac
A.  *April*

Q.  Name something slippery
A.  *A conman*

Q.  Name a famous Scotsman
A.  *Jock*

Q.  Name something a blind man might use
A.  *A sword*

Q.  Name a domestic animal
A.  *Leopard*

Q.  Name a part of the body beginning with 'N'
A.  *Knee*

Q.  Name something you open other than a door
A.  *Your bowels*

# You've gotta laugh

President Bush was awakened one night at the White House by an urgent call from the Pentagon.

'Mr President,' said Secretary of Defense Donald Rumsfeld, barely able to contain himself, 'I've got good news and bad news for you.'

'OK, Don,' muttered the President. 'Hit me with it. The bad news first.'

'The bad news, sir,' said Rumsfeld, 'is that we've been invaded by aliens from another planet.'

'That's pretty bad, Don,' said the President. 'Now give me the good news.'

'The good news, sir,' announced Rumsfeld, 'is that they eat only reporters and Democrats and they pee oil.'

# Hark who's talking about the fame

**Andy Warhol:**
'In the future, everybody will be famous for fifteen minutes.'

**Fred Allen:**
'A celebrity is a person who works hard all his life to become well known, then wears dark glasses to avoid being recognised.'

**Oscar Wilde:**
*(arriving at United States customs)*
'I have nothing to declare but my genius.'

**Henry Kissinger:**
'The nice thing about being a celebrity is that when you bore people, they think it's their fault.'

**Walt Disney:**
'Fancy being remembered around the world for the creation of a mouse!'

**Napoleon Bonaparte:**
'Glory is fleeting, but obscurity is for ever.'

**Victor Hugo:**
'Popularity? It is glory's small change.'

**Alan Ayckbourn:**
'I go in and out of fashion like a double-breasted suit.'

**Tommy Docherty:**
*(on a temperamental footballer)*
'He is a legend in his own half-time.'

**Fran Lebowitz:**
'The best fame is a writer's fame. It is enough to get a table at a good restaurant, but not enough that you get interrupted when you eat.'

**Norman Collier:**
'I was famous once. It was on the Thursday before last.'

**W. Somerset Maugham:**
'Being famous is like being given a string of pearls. It's very nice, but after a while you begin to wonder if they are real or cultured.'

**P. J. O'Rourke:**
'You can't shame or humiliate modern celebrities. What used to be called shame and humiliation is now called publicity.'

**Sting:**
'Celebrity is good for kick-starting ideas, but often celebrity is a lead weight around your neck. It's like you pointing at the moon, but people are looking at your finger.'

**Eric Morecambe:**
'Fame is about walking into a restaurant and having people laugh just because you've come through the door. And they will still laugh when they see me send the food back because the laughing waiter has got my order wrong. What a laugh!'

**Norman Wisdom:**
'Don't laugh at me because I'm a fool.'

**Jimmy Greaves:**
'I suppose the fact that I had my first autobiography published when I was twenty meant I was famous, but I had hardly lived, apart from travel from one football ground to another. But I made up for it later.'

**John Lennon:**
'I would much rather be famous for my work than for my play.'

**Marlene Dietrich:**
'My fame is such that people seem to think I am a myth.'

**Madonna:**
'I won't be happy until I'm as famous as God.'

**Lord Byron:**
'What is fame? The advantage of being known by people of whom you know nothing and for whom you care as little.'

**Oprah Winfrey:**
'If you come to fame not understanding who you are, it will define who you are.'

**Stan Boardman:**
'I'm famous for causing an uproar by saying "Fokker" on television. Now loads say the real word and nobody bats an eyelid. How times change.'

**Muhammad Ali:**
'I'm so famous that even in Russia more know of me than their own president.'

**Frank Carson:**
'It's nice to be remembered and talked about after you're dead. I hope I'm there to see it.'

**Julia Roberts:**
'I don't think I realised that the cost of fame is that it's open season on every moment of your life.'

**Bob Monkhouse:**
'Fame is a fickle mistress who is likely to go off and have an affair with somebody else just as you think the relationship is permanent.'

**Dirk Bogarde:**
'Fame means goodbye to privacy. It's a big price to pay.'

**Dudley Moore:**
'My Aunt Gladys was well known in Dagenham for sleeping with a lot of strange men. She enjoyed her fame.'

**Bette Midler:**
'When you become famous you think, "Is this all there is?"'

**Ken Dodd:**
'Fame is being able to pick your nose in public and considered eccentric rather than having a dirty habit.'

**Johnny Depp:**
'I'm shy, paranoid, whatever word you want to use. I hate fame. I've done everything I can to avoid it.'

**Kenneth More:**
'Better to have lasting sanity than lasting fame.'

**David Niven:**
'Being famous is fine provided it is accompanied by lots of noughts on your pay cheque.'

**Chris Rock:**
'I love being famous. It's almost like being white.'

**Dolly Parton:**
'I would prefer to be remembered for the songs I've written and sung than for the size of my assets.'

**Brad Pitt:**
'Fame is a bitch, man.'

# 7 This Sporting Laugh

Anybody who kindly read *Football My Arse!* will know that I am a sports nut. I collect sports stories like other people collect stamps, and now I have another chance to stick them in a book and share them with you.

My first love – even ahead of football – is world heavyweight championship boxing. I have always been hooked on the heavy mob, and my interest goes way back to the days when the Brockton Blockbuster Rocky Marciano ruled the world like a one-man demolition force.

Rocky, who remains the only world heavyweight champion to have retired without a single defeat to blemish his 49–0 record, made a comeback of sorts six months before his death in a plane crash.

He was persuaded to face Muhammad Ali in a computer-programmed fight in front of the film cameras. Every move was choreographed, and they filmed four different endings.

They plonked a wig on Rocky's bald head, and hid his bulging paunch in a pair of specially tailored shorts that acted as a sort of corset. Rocky talked like Marlon 'I coulda been a contender' Brando in *On the Waterfront*. 'Hey, ya know summmthin'?' Rocky said as the make-up artist fitted his hairpiece. 'This rug cost more than I got for my first professional fight.'

Marciano died the day before his forty-sixth birthday on 31 August

1969 without knowing the result of the phantom fight. A week later the film was released with the version showing him stopping Ali in the tenth round.

Ali said later: 'I went along with it out of respect for Rocky's memory, but the truth is that at my peak he could not have hit me with a handful of rice.'

I beg to differ on that one. For several years I have been trying to get TV companies interested in letting me show how and why Marciano earned the right to be called 'The Greatest' ahead of Ali. The Rock's record says it all: forty-nine fights, forty-nine wins, and he did not duck any of the top fighters around at the time. Any TV company executive reading this and wanting a contentious and fascinating fight programme, please get in touch with me. I am deadly serious about this because I feel Rocky's reputation has been short-changed because of Ali's clever use of the gab as well as his jab.

Ali had a quote for every occasion, but even he was almost lost for words when he heard the size of the alimony cheque he would have to pay his first wife, Sonji, following their divorce in 1967.

'I'm the only one to beat him,' said Sonji. 'He's going to remember that every day for the next ten years while he's making the payments.'

When he got over the initial shock, Ali said: 'I'm having to pay so much money that they've even named the payments after me – *Ali-money*!'

Anybody who knows their boxing will recall one of Ali's most famous fights, just after he had changed his name from Cassius Clay. He had a bitter championship showdown contest with the human skyscraper Ernie Terrell, who refused to call him by his new Muslim name. Throughout the fight Ali taunted Terrell with the question, 'What's mah name?' A few days later Tottenham were playing Fulham at White Hart Lane when Spurs schemer Terry Venables and Fulham defender Fred Callaghan got involved in some fisticuffs that led to them both being ordered off. As they were sparring and threatening to throw punches at each other, a

Which one of these will you want at your side if you're up a creek without a paddle? Sir Steve Redgrave is one of the most incredible sportsmen of all time. Five Olympic rowing gold medals across a span of 20 years. He really knows how to push the boat out.

voice from the terraces pleaded: 'For f***'s sake, Fred, tell him his name . . .'

Back in those days when he was known as Clay, the young Ali was training in London for his first fight with 'Our Enery' Cooper. This was in 1963, and Ali was working out in promoter Jack Solomons' famous gymnasium opposite the Windmill Theatre in London's West End.

As Ali thumped the punchbag he became aware of somebody watching him with intense interest. The man would not take his eyes off him, and was standing closer than the usual idle spectator. It got to the point where Ali was becoming unsettled by the man's fanatical stare. He was about to shout one of his acid insults at him when it was quietly pointed out that the uninvited guest was the notorious London gangster Ronnie Kray (the madder of the twins), and that it would be unwise to make an enemy of him. Clay absorbed the information, and then shouted, 'Hey man, *you're* the Greatest.'

My pal Norman Giller worked as a publicist on the midnight fight in Munich in 1976, when Ali defended the world title against British lionheart Richard Dunn. As a ticket-selling gimmick, he arranged for the English hypnotist Romark to go to Munich to put Dunn under a hypnotic spell to help his victory bid. This was the same Romark who decided he could use hypnotic powers to drive himself blindfolded for a mile through London. He got fifty yards when he drove into the back of a parked car. Just his luck that it was a police car. You can imagine the look on the copper's face when he saw that he had been rear-ended by a driver wearing a blindfold!

Unbeknown to Norman, Romark had suffered a stroke a few months before the Ali–Dunn fight that had left him with one eye lower than the other and his speech slightly slurred.

So you have the picture. Romark, a total eccentric, with his face contorted, in Germany to help Richard Dunn. Only Romark would have taken it upon himself to go beyond his brief and confront Ali. He was convinced he could hypnotise the Champ.

Romark suddenly challenged Ali before the weigh-in. Ali fell to his knees laughing uncontrollably as Romark jumped in front of him, his eyes bulging like Marty Feldman on speed. 'You are doomed to defeat tonight,' the hypnotist shouted in his slurred voice. 'D-o-o-m-e-d.'

As Ali rolled on the floor, almost choking with laughter, Romark realised he had failed with that part of his plan. But there was still Richard Dunn. Later that afternoon, he tucked Richard up in bed in his hotel room and told him the story of Cinderella. As the Bradford hero slipped off into sleep, he kept telling him his fists were made of iron. Richard later confided that he had feigned going to sleep 'just to get rid of the nutter'.

When the Dunn entourage got to the stadium for the fight, they were annoyed to find an American TV crew in their dressing-room. Manager George Biddles ordered them out. While the cameraman continued to focus on Richard, his trainer and father-in-law Jimmy Devanney turned off the dressing-room lights.

But this backfired because Richard was now sitting in a darkened dressing-room. He found himself staring at a TV monitor on the wall that was showing live pictures of Muhammad Ali in his dressing-room telling the American television public what he intended to do to his challenger.

Dunn put up a brave, beyond-the-call-of-duty performance before being stopped in five rounds by Ali, who by then was past his dazzling peak.

When he returned to the Munich hotel at 3 a.m., Dunn was met by a posse of hard-boiled British pressmen who were moved to applaud his brave stand.

Romark, with tears streaming down his face, pushed his way through the reporters and cuddled Dunn. 'I let you down, Richard,' he sobbed. 'I made your fists turn into iron – but I forgot about your chin!'

You couldn't make it up.

Now for some of my more favourite sporting anecdotes, and continuing the boxing theme . . .

After Mike Tyson had been disqualified for biting a lump out of Evander Holyfield's ear during their heavyweight war in 1997, the Hollywood Wax Museum transferred their model of Tyson from the 'Sports Hall of Fame' to the 'Chamber of Horrors' – placing him alongside Hannibal Lecter!

Jack Dempsey, who would have plenty of support in his claim to being the hardest-hitting heavyweight champion of all time, was once asked by a young prospect for boxing advice. 'Well, son, some night you'll catch a punch between the eyes and all of a sudden you'll see three opponents in the ring,' said the old champ. 'Pick out the one in the middle and hit him as hard as you can, because as sure as eggs is eggs he's the one who hit you.'

Jerry Quarry, former world heavyweight title challenger, knocked out British champion Jack Bodell in just sixty-four seconds at Wembley in 1971. In the dressing-room after his instant hit, Quarry told reporters: 'I was warned that Bodell was big and awkward, and he was. He was very big and he fell very awkwardly.'

A PGA golf tournament was in full swing in the United States, and the great Arnold Palmer was preparing to drive from the tee. The television commentator decided to share some fascinating trivia about Arnie that had viewers falling about laughing. 'One of the reasons Arnie is playing so well is because of a little superstition he has,' revealed the commentator. 'Before each tournament his wife takes out his balls and kisses them.'

The modern golfing master Tiger Woods was once introduced to pop singer Christina Aguilera.

'So pleased to meet you,' gushed Tiger. 'I have all your CDs and am a great fan.'

Christina graciously accepted the compliment, and replied: 'Thank you so much. I just wish I knew more about your tennis career.'

After the first of his victories in the US Masters it was reported that the then President Bill Clinton telephoned Tiger and said: 'Congratulations. We must make up a foursome one day. And another time we might play some golf.'

I don't believe it for a second, but why let facts spoil a good story!

During one of the US Opens, Tiger came out of an on-course portaloo to be greeted by rapturous applause from his huge gallery of fans. He said as an aside to his caddie: 'They even applaud me for being potty trained!'

Lee Trevino, the great walkie-talkie Texan golfer, realised his caddie in a charity event at Las Vegas was a novice when he drove off the first tee and asked how far he was from the green. 'About three blocks' came the reply.

Ian Woosnam was having one of his less illustrious rounds early in his career as a professional golfer. He had spent more time in the woods than David Bellamy, and was struggling to break 80.

There was no chance of him making the cut. As he stood ankle deep in the rough at the seventeenth, he asked his caddie: 'What d'you recommend I take now?'

'The next train home,' said the caddie.

Prince Andrew has caught the golf bug, and I wonder whether he will become as fanatical a player as his great-uncle, the Duke of Windsor, who – when he was Prince of Wales – was coached by the maestro Henry Cotton.

'I was playing a round with the Prince at Gleneagles when we were reduced to helpless laughter,' Cotton recalled. 'The Prince was crouching, trying to work out his line for a long putt, and he asked his caddie's advice.

'"If I were you, sir," he said in a thick Irish accent, "I'd hit it slightly straight."'

Singer Andy Williams, a golf fanatic, was having one of those rounds when nothing would go right during a charity tournament in Atlanta. He was continually in and out of the woods, spent more time in the bunker than Hitler and rarely saw the fairway.

On reaching the eighteenth green he asked his caddie: 'What should I do with this putt?'

The caddie advised: 'Keep it as low as possible.'

Comedian Bob Hope was playing in a charity golf match with President Gerald Ford, who was notorious for slicing off the tee and hitting spectators. Asked how the President was doing, Hope cracked: 'He's two bodyguards under par. To get his score we look down the fairway and count the wounded.'

Doug Sanders will always be remembered for missing a sitter of a putt that would have won him the British Open in 1970 (he went on to lose in a play-off to Jack Nicklaus). He also had putting problems in the 1968 Masters when he played magnificent golf everywhere but on the greens. At the end of his round his caddie Walter 'Cricket' Pritchett said: 'Nice work, Mr Doug. You've just managed to turn a perfect 64 into a 72!'

Playing in an LPGA tournament in 1995, Elaine Johnson hooked a shot off the fairway. The ball hit a tree and bounced back towards her, coming to rest in her bra! After discussions with the rules official, Elaine elected to take a two-point penalty and a drop rather than play it 'where it lies'. She played that hole under bra . . . or was it a double bogey?

In Colin Montgomerie's overweight days, the temperamental Scot was playing a tournament in the United States and was walking back through a gallery of abusive American fans who were giving him a bad time. This was in the period when he was spitefully nicknamed Mrs Doubtfire.

One persistent spectator ran after Monty shouting, 'Hey, Montgomerie.'

Monty ignored him and kept walking.

'Hey, Montgomerie,' the fan shouted again.

Monty continued to cock a deaf 'un.

The spectator decided on a new approach. 'Hey, Mr Montgomerie, sir . . .'

The good manners paid dividends, and as Monty stopped and turned the spectator shouted: 'Nice tits.'

To his great credit, Monty just shook his head and continued his walk. Me, I would have taken a seven iron to the feller's big mouth.

**Golfer Colin Montgomerie was cruelly nicknamed Mrs Doubtfire by spectators in the United States. But he had the last laugh on them with his brilliant performances in the Ryder Cup. I reckon those alleged golf fans made complete tits of themselves.**

What odds on a hole in one? American professional golfer Harry Gonder was convinced that a scratch golfer should be able to land one in a given number of shots. He filled a bucket with balls and, with two officials in tow as witnesses, he went to the tee at the 160-yard third hole to test his theory. He estimated that it would not take him more than half an hour to get an ace. He bombarded the flag with balls, and came within five inches of the hole on his eighty-sixth shot.

He then took a break for lunch after failing to get the elusive hole in one with 941 shots. His fifty-fifth shot on his restart came to rest within three inches of the flag, but still no ace.

He continued right through the afternoon and long into the night under the glare of car headlights. Substitute witnesses were called in to replace the exhausted original judges. Finally, at three o'clock in the morning, after sixteen hours of hitting and hoping, he had to concede defeat.

Harry had played a total of 1,817 shots without getting a hole in one.

What a load of balls.

Three months later, playing in competition, he holed out with a seven iron.

The British Open Golf Championship committee tightened their entry rules after Maurice Flitcroft, a forty-six-year-old crane driver from Barrow-in-Furness, carded a record 121 strokes in the first qualifying round at Formby in Lancashire in 1976. 'I could have done with a bit more practice,' he said.

Martin Johnson, Jonny Wilkinson, Matt Dawson and co. were celebrating England's dramatic last-minute Rugby World Cup final victory over Australia when their famous fan Prince Harry came into the dressing-room. Dawson revealed: 'Harry said, "Just want you to know, chaps, that my nan has sent me a text to say she wants to give you all a party at Buck House!" We were all gobsmacked that the Queen could send text messages.'

Gareth Edwards, one of the all-time great scrum-halves, listened with a straight face as Welsh team coach John Dawes outlined his plan to introduce codewords at a training session before a match against England.

'When you want the left-side flanker to make a break, the codeword should start with a "P",' said Dawes. 'If you want a break on the right side, use a codeword beginning with "S."'

Dawes tossed the ball to Edwards who put it into the scrum and shouted: 'Psychology!'

Dr A. J. (Tony) O'Reilly, who became the billionaire boss of Heinz, was the pin-up boy of Irish rugby during his playing career as a crash-bang-wallop right wing. He was playing in a match for Leinster when he dislocated his shoulder during a typical dash for the line.

'The physio was summoned,' recalled O'Reilly, a born raconteur. 'He was a local GP, and as he took a firm grip on my shoulder I could not help but yell with the sudden pain.

'"Come on O'Reilly," the GP said. "I've just delivered a baby and the mother didn't make half as much fuss."

'"Maybe not," I said. "But you weren't trying to push it back in!"'

O'Reilly, who turned down offers from Hollywood to concentrate on his business career, was playing in a match for Ireland against England at Twickenham during which Phil Horrocks-Taylor cleverly dummied past Irish stand-off Mick English to score a try.

'Horrocks went this way,' said O'Reilly, 'Taylor went that way, and poor Mick was left holding the hyphen.'

Bill Beaumont was England skipper the day that the well-endowed Erica Roe made her headline-hitting streak at Twickenham in 1982. 'Hey, Bill,'

scrum-half Steve Smith said as Erica bounced across the pitch, 'there's a bird just run on with your bum on her chest.'

I could not resist including these snippets of Radio Five Live commentary I heard from Jonathan Agnew during England's celebrations after clinching the Ashes in the summer of 2005 . . .

'Freddie Flintoff's eyes are barely open and his tie is similarly barely held together. He has clearly been sampling the best that No. 10 Downing Street has to offer . . .

'The players are heading onto the pitch led by a steward. I can see Duncan Fletcher, Michael Vaughan and co. I was going to say Freddie Flintoff is striding across the pitch at Lord's but that's probably a bit generous.'

Then there was this cracker during a call-in from a bloke calling himself 'Graham, of Manchester':

'I'd promised to run nude through the streets of Manchester if England won the Ashes and this morning was true to my word. I ran pretty quickly and unfortunately my mother turned up. I think my work colleagues think it's idiotic for a managing director of a company to be doing this.'

The marvellous Matthew Hoggard gave an insight into the liquid extent of England's Ashes victory celebrations when he revealed the morning after the night before: 'I said last night I only expected to see three men and his dog come along to this parade of the Ashes Urn, but it seems the entire country has backed us.

'I remember having a few beers last night and then it all went a bit hazy. I passed out on the bedroom floor and my wife covered me with a dressing gown. I could not even manage to speak!'

Matthew did manage to speak later in the day . . . to Prime Minister Tony Blair. This was how he recalled it:

'My memory is blurred, but I seem to recall a big red thing – so I guess we must have taken a bus to No. 10 Downing Street. Tony popped in for a glass of – what did they offer us? – *pineapple juice!* You can guess what we made them think of that, and somebody hustled up some beer. As we left Downing Street there were a lot of photographers waiting outside No. 10. The Prime Minister said, "What do they want?" So I looked at him and said, "A photo, you knob!" Oh dear! I was a bit out of order, but he took it in good spirit.'

England batsmen Allan Lamb and Robin Smith looked up in amazement when two biplanes started to buzz the pitch as they batted against Queensland at Carrara during the 1990–91 tour Down Under.

Smith reacted by putting his bat to his shoulder and mimed taking shots at the invaders, not for one moment guessing that it was his England team-mates David Gower and John Morris flying overhead.

'Biggles' Gower and Morris had hired two Tiger Moths at a nearby flying school.

Gower, one of the most elegant stroke-makers ever to play Test cricket, later revealed that he was disappointed that he had not quite completed his planned operation. 'I had wanted to bombard the pitch with waterbombs,' he said, 'but it didn't quite work out.'

MCC chiefs fined Gower and Morris a thousand quid each. I reckon they should have given them medals for bringing a smile to the face of sport.

Keith Miller, an all-rounder with few peers and a larger-than-life playboy of a character, was leading out the New South Wales team at the start of the first morning's play when an alert member did his sums, and said: 'Skip, we've got twelve players.'

Miller hardly broke stride as he shouted over his shoulder, 'One of you had better f*** off.'

Dennis Lillee, arguably the finest of all fast bowlers, was fiercely competitive, but he always found time for some banter with his favourite umpire, Dickie Bird. Once, after Dickie had turned down his loud LBW appeal, Dennis said: 'I think your eyesight's going, Dickie.'

'No,' replied Dickie, 'it's *your* eyesight that's going. I'm the ice-cream seller.'

Towards the end of his career, when he was combining cricket with pantomime appearances, Ian Botham rapped a batsman on the pads and shouted: 'Owzat!'

Dickie Bird responded with a panto-style shout: 'Oh no he isn't!'

Botham reckoned he got some of the worst reviews of any panto star. He appeared in *Babes in the Wood* and one critic wrote: 'Botham was more wooden than any tree in the forest.'

In the early days of mobile telephones, Dickie Bird was standing in the middle umpiring a match at Northampton when Allan Lamb came in to bat. He handed Dickie one of the new-fangled phones and said, 'Meant to leave this in the dressing-room. Look after it for me, Dickie.'

Five minutes later the telephone rang, and Dickie jumped a foot in the air. Lambie, at the other end, shouted: 'Answer it, Dickie, and tell them to ring back.'

Dickie did as he was asked, and fumed when he learned it was Ian Botham on the line, asking him the score.

A cricketer who could match even Botham and Lamb as a prankster was former Hampshire skipper Colin Ingleby-Mackenzie, whose cavalier approach to the game (and life) is best summed up by his famous quote: 'I always insist that my players are in bed before ten o'clock during a match. After all, play starts at eleven-thirty!'

During his playing days with Yorkshire, Dickie Bird was shaping up to face a ball against Hampshire at Bournemouth when he heard the sound of a radio horserace commentary. He looked towards the slips to find Old Etonian Ingleby-Mackenzie with a transistor to his ear. 'Hope I'm not breaking your concentration, old chap,' said Ingers. 'I've got a few bob riding on a nag.'

Ingleby-Mackenzie's image as a lovable rascal became widely known when he gave an extraordinary tongue-in-cheek interview on BBC TV's *Junior Sportsview*.

The earnest, po-faced interviewer clearly knew nothing about cricket, and Inglers – who had just skippered Hampshire to an unlikely County Championship – could not resist the temptation to send him up. Their exchange went like this:

'Mr Ingleby-Mackenzie, to what do you attribute Hampshire's success?'

'Oh, wine, women and song, I should say.'

'But don't you have certain rules, discipline, helpful hints for the younger viewer?'

'Well, everyone in bed in time for breakfast, I suppose, and play hard on and off the pitch.'

'Yes, thank you. Perhaps we could take a look in the dressing-room?'

'Certainly, if you don't mind me wandering about in the nude.'

The director quickly ordered a return to the studio.

Ingers passed on to the great pavilion in the sky while I was putting this book together. You will not see his like again. He was a throwback to the old-style sportsmen who played purely for the fun and joy of it.

Back to Dennis Lillee. He was so furious when the umpires ruled that he could not use his revolutionary aluminium bat in the Perth Test against England in 1979 that he hurled it farther than he had been hitting the ball. In the second innings he scored nineteen with a traditional willow blade before the headline writers got the special wicket they had been waiting for: 'Lillee, caught Willey, bowled Dilley.'

Even more hilarious was this descriptive piece of commentary from Brian Johnston during *Test Match Special*'s coverage of an England–West Indies match: 'The bowler's Holding, the batsman's Willey.'

John Snow, Sussex and England fast bowler, came roaring in to bowl to Leicestershire batsman Paul Marner, who went on to his back foot to hook what was a loose full toss. As his bat connected the 'ball' disintegrated.

Snow and the rest of the Sussex team were on their knees in helpless laughter. He had bowled a round bar of red soap. Snow said to the local newspaper reporter that it was the start of a 'clean-up cricket' campaign.

Lester Piggott was not only the king of jockeys but the master of the one-line put-down. He was once approached by trainer Jeremy Tree, who told him: 'I've got to speak to my old school this weekend, Lester, and tell them all I know about racing. What d'you suggest I say?'

After appearing to give the question careful thought, Lester said: 'Tell them you've got the flu.'

On another occasion Lester was flying in a helicopter with an owner who wore a monogram on his handmade shirt. 'Why d'you have your initials on your shirt?' Lester asked. 'In case you forget who you are?'

Few punters ever lost their shirt on Lester.

Willie Carson was racing towards the winning post at Pontefract with what he thought was a comfortable lead when he suddenly sensed a challenge coming on his outside. He called for a greater effort from his mount, but still he was aware of a shadow looming on his shoulder.

'I drove my horse even harder and was relieved to get past the post in first place,' said Willie. 'Then I looked behind me to see how close the other horse was. I couldn't see a thing. I'd spent the last couple of furlongs racing my own shadow. The official winning distance was fifteen lengths.'

It was Carson who told the true story of the English punter who drowned his sorrows after losing his money on Generous in the 1991 Arc de Triomphe at Longchamp. He was helped aboard a London-bound charter flight in a legless condition. It was only when he started to sober up somewhere over the White Cliffs of Dover that he realised he had driven to Paris.

Snooker maestro Dennis Taylor was amazed to see a letter sent to the BBC presenter David Vine. It was from an elderly lady who claimed to have worked out why the matches in snooker lasted so long. Taylor, of course, was winner of the most epic encounter of them all, when eighteen million viewers stayed up to the small hours to see his victory over Steve Davis. He says the woman wrote: 'The problem is the man with the white gloves keeps on taking the potted balls out of the pockets and putting them back on the table.'

Jimmy 'The Whirlwind' White used to spend more time at the snooker table than at his school desk when he was a kid, and by the time he was thirteen could pick up more in one side bet than his schoolteacher could earn in a year. 'It got to the stage', recalled Jimmy, 'when my teacher did a deal with me. He told me that provided I came to school for the morning lessons he would let me off in the afternoons to play snooker. He told my parents that it was the only way he could guarantee ever seeing me!'

Steve Davis has played up to his 'interesting' image but has in fact got a nicely developed line in dry humour. He once reduced a camera crew and director to helpless laughter when recording a snooker instruction programme.

'This is the ideal place to hit the pack with the cue ball when breaking off,' he said, then gave the demonstration.

The ball glanced off the pack, ran down to the bottom cushion and spun into a corner pocket.

Steve looked into the camera and said: 'Here endeth the lesson and Steve Davis's television career.'

John Virgo, famous for his *Big Break* appearances and impressions at the table, was competing in a televised match against Cliff 'The Grinder' Thorburn when he was played into a virtually inescapable snooker. John, who is now one of the voices of BBC snooker, shook his head as he studied the balls and said: 'I've not yet quite mastered an impression of Houdini.'

Björn Borg had the distant help of his grandfather when he won the French Open in 1979. His seventy-three-year-old granddad listened to the final on the radio while sitting on a fishing boat near Sweden's Kattilo Island. He spat nervously into the water when Björn won the first point, and he decided with illogical superstition that this had helped his grandson. From then on he spat after every winning point, and had a bone-dry throat by the time Björn had beaten Victor Pecci in four sets.

Borg was in spitting distance of the greatest tennis career ever.

John 'Superbrat' McEnroe surpassed himself on his way to defeat by Stefan Edberg in the 1992 Wimbledon Championships. He swore at a linesman six times in ten seconds, an outburst that was picked up by an ITN microphone. This is a censored version of

You cannot be serious! John McEnroe was one of the most obnoxious yet at the same time most exciting tennis players ever to step on to a tennis court. Now – in the TV commentary box – he talks almost as good a game as he played, and without the bleep-bleep language.

what millions of shocked TV viewers heard: 'Blank, you stupid blanker. Good blanking call, you son of a blanking bitch.' It cost McEnroe a maximum $10,000 fine, or $1,000 a second.

Jimmy Connors, the big-hearted street fighter of the tennis courts, was in the McEnroe class with his tongue during the 1992 US Open. Following a disputed line call, he yelled at the umpire: 'You son of a bitch. Get out of that chair and get a job. I'm out here playing my butt off at thirty-nine, and you're pulling that crap.'

Anyone for tennis?

American comedy actor Ben Stiller, visiting the UK to appear in an episode of the hilarious *Extras* series with Ricky Gervais, revealed that he was into the new world of extreme sports. He described how he was once persuaded to join some friends on an extreme adventure. 'I have a buddy who's a triathlete,' he explained, 'and he said, "Come on. Go on a night mountain biking trip with us." So I got myself a bike and joined him and three of his friends, who were, I quickly realised, sort of super-jock guys. As soon as I rode up to join them I immediately knew I was in trouble because they started chuckling. Apparently I had a girl's mountain bike. I didn't realise.

'They started putting on shin pads and elbow pads and spine guards . . . and I'm in the spandex . . . and then they started putting on these helmets, like these helmets that have miner's lights on them. "What", I thought, "am I doing here?"

'We started going along this dirt path by the ocean and I got quite a rush from that. The moon was out, and I was filled with a sense of total freedom. We're going one mile, two miles, three miles. I'm kind of getting exhausted but I'm excited that I'm part of this thing. We get to five miles and I'm asking, "How much longer, guys?"

'We get to the top of this hill and everybody gets off their bikes. I'm like, "Yes! This is good, we did it." Then they start checking their gears and pulling out energy food bars and preparing. And I said, "What's going on?" and they said, "Well, we're at the trail head. We're ready to start."

'"God," I thought to myself, "we've done all that work just to get to the start!"

'One guy, who's super-serious, just looks at me and says, "Whatever happens, don't fight the mountain." I have no idea what it means but it scared the crap out of me.

'As they started down the hill – a 75-degree descent – I found myself falling behind. But then this adrenaline kicked in – a sort of fear, I guess – and I started going real good. I could hear them up ahead and I was beginning to feel every part of me disintegrating with all the effort. One of them yelled out, "No brunch! No brunch!" And I'm like, "All right, yeah. This is some biking term. Like, we're going so well, there's momentum happening, we're not gonna stop to eat the energy bars." So I'm like, "Yeah! No brunch! No brunch!"

'So I looked up and there's this three-foot-thick tree-trunk flying at me. And you know they say when an accident happens everything slows down and you go in slow motion and somehow your instincts kick in and you do whatever it takes to save yourself in that moment? That didn't happen. So I slammed right into it and as I came to, they were all sort of staring at me like, "Man, didn't you hear? Low branch! Low branch!"'

The baseball commentator at Illinois radio station was working from a telegraph service, delivering his 'live' on-air descriptions from a downtown studio as he tore each running report from the wire machine. There was a sudden break in transmission, and the commentator decided to ad-lib, creating for his listeners his imaginative version of what he thought might be happening in the 1933 World Series.

The next day's papers revealed that the action had been nowhere near where his mouth was. The commentator was a young, aspiring actor called Ronald 'The Great Communicator' Reagan.

Jim Thorpe, a full-blooded Sac Indian from Oklahoma, won both the pentathlon and the decathlon at the 1912 Olympics in Stockholm. The King of Sweden told him: 'Sir, you are the greatest athlete in the world.' Thorpe replied, 'Thanks, King.'

Helen Stephens and Stanislawa Walasiewicz dominated women's sprinting during the 1930s. Walasiewicz, born in Poland but raised in the United States, was Olympic 100 metres champion in 1932, and took the silver behind Stephens in the 1936 Berlin Olympics.

Stephens was accused by Polish officials of being more man than woman, and she took six sex tests to disprove the allegation. She retired with an unbeaten sprint record, while her arch-rival Walasiewicz – who changed her name to Stella Walsh – continued her career, during which she set eleven world records and won forty-one USA sprint titles.

We now zoom forward in time to 4 December 1980. Forty-one years after hanging up her spikes, Stella was out shopping at a Cleveland store when she was innocently caught in the cross-fire during a robbery attempt. She was shot dead.

An autopsy revealed that the athletics heroine of the thirties had male sexual organs. The Polish officials had levelled their accusations at the wrong athlete.

More recently, a German gentleman called Hermann Ratjen confessed that he had competed in the 1936 Olympics in the *women's* high jump. He was entered under the name Dora Ratjen, having been forced by the Nazi Youth Movement to masquerade as a woman.

This was a desperate attempt by the Nazis to prove their women were the best jumpers in the world. Hermann failed them, finishing fourth. Perhaps a jackboot up the arse might have helped him.

Defending the Olympic middleweight championship he had won in 1920, British boxer Harry Mallin was involved in an extraordinary incident in the 1924 quarter-finals against Frenchman Roger Brousse. In the final round, when seemingly ahead on points, Mallin was bitten on the chest by Brousse during a close-quarters clinch.

Mallin attempted to protest to the referee, but because of language difficulties could not make himself understood.

Brousse was awarded a controversial points decision, but following a complaint from a neutral Swedish official who had seen the biting incident, the boxing committee held an inquiry. They studied the tell-tale marks on Mallin's chest, disqualified Brousse and reversed the decision.

Mallin, a London policeman, went on to retain his title by out-pointing fellow Brit John Elliott in the final. British champion from 1919 to 1923, Mallin went through his career of more than two hundred amateur contests without a single defeat . . . even by a hungry fighter!

Seconds out for a true story from Paddy Byrne, who for forty years worked in boxing as a manager, matchmaker, trainer, cornerman, agent and cuts man. 'I took a boxer to Denmark for an eight-round contest', he recalled. 'We flew from London to Copenhagen, a flight that took little more than an hour. I thought my boxer was in good shape and could not understand why he was puffing and blowing after just three rounds.

'As he flopped down on his stool at the end of the third round, I asked: "What's wrong with you?"

'He shrugged his shoulders and said with deadly seriousness: "I'm suffering from jet lag."'

Irish boxer Pat Desmond was taking a hammering in an all-Ireland heavyweight championship contest and went down on his knees in his own corner in the third round. His second shouted, 'Don't get up until nine, Pat . . . Don't get up 'til nine.'

Still kneeling, Pat shouted back: 'And what time is it now?'

Comedy actor Sid James, *Carry On* star and brilliant straight man to Tony Hancock, was feeling unwell one morning and booked himself in to see a private doctor. He was given a thorough examination, and advised to give up smoking and cut right down on his heavy drinking. This is the way Sid told the story: 'As I was leaving the doctor's surgery his receptionist gave me a bill for fifty quid. "That's for the doctor's advice," she said. I told her, "Well I owe him nothing because I'm not taking his advice."'

You might be wondering what a Sid James anecdote is doing in this chapter about sports celebrities. Well, Sid claimed to have been a professional middleweight boxer before leaving his native South Africa to seek the gold he'd been told paved the streets of London.

Asked why he gave up boxing – and this was when Muhammad Ali was first starting to make a name for himself – Sid explained: 'I realised I had got it all wrong. I was floating like a bee and stinging like a butterfly. So I switched to acting. Punchlines don't hurt your hooter as much.'

The following true story sounds as if it could have come out of an episode of John Sullivan's *Only Fools and Horses*. It was the height of the Cold War, and Canada's world champion ice hockey team travelled to Moscow to play Russia in a Summit Series. The players and coaches were warned to mind what they said about tactics in their hotel rooms because of bugging. They took the warning so seriously that a secret sweep of their hotel rooms was ordered. Sure enough, they found what they were convinced was a bug.

It was in the form of a round piece of metal embedded in the floor, and hidden under a rug. The Canadian coaches worked together to dig it out, and suddenly heard a crashing sound beneath them. They had released the screws anchoring a chandelier that crashed on to the banqueting-room floor below.

You can almost hear Del Boy: 'Ready when you are, Granddad.'

Martin Brundle, once a top-flight Formula One race ace and now an excellent ITV commentator, tells a lovely story of his early days on the circuit as a driver. He arrived in Rio de Janeiro for a Grand Prix, and was astonished to find experienced American driver Danny Sullivan pushing away a posse of beautiful Brazilian girls. 'I wondered what was wrong with him,' said Brundle.

It all became clear when Sullivan quietly told him: 'They come at you in threes. One to kiss you . . . one to hug you . . . and the third to pick your back pocket.'

Niki Lauda suffered horrific facial burns before being dragged from a blazing Grand Prix car. On the point of an amazing comeback, he was asked by a television interviewer: 'Tell us, Niki, do you have any burning ambitions left?'

'The Olympic Games can no more lose money,' Montreal Mayor Jean Drapeau declared after winning the right to host the 1976 Olympics, 'than a man can have a baby.' After the Olympics, Montreal was left with a spectacular new velodrome (torn down a few years later), a massive stadium (whose retractable roof never functioned properly), and a municipal debt of one billion dollars. Even to this day, the good people of Montreal are continuing to pay off the debt through their rates.

Are you listening, Ken Livingstone? Bet there will be some lord-mayoring if the London Games of 2012 go into the red.

Ever wondered why the marathon is the odd distance of 26 miles 385 yards? It used to be exactly 26 miles until the 1908 Olympics in London, which brings me to the story of Dorando Pietri, who remains the most famous runner never to have won an Olympic marathon.

The spindly legged little candymaker from Capri was the first man into London's White City Stadium after exactly 26 miles in the 1908 Games. He then had the little matter of an extra 385 yards to go to reach the finishing line opposite the Royal Box, where Queen Alexandra was waiting to greet the winner. It was a bridge too far.

Dorando, in his white vest and knickerbockers and with a white knotted handkerchief on his head, suddenly slowed to a drunken walk as he reached the cinder track. What should have been a lap of glory turned into a nightmare journey as he reeled on rubber legs, not knowing which way to turn for the finishing line.

Doctors and officials crowded anxiously around him as the Italian crumpled slowly to the ground like a puppet that has had its strings cut. Four times he collapsed, and four times willing hands helped him up, finally guiding him through the tape.

American John Hayes was second across the line, finishing under his own steam several minutes later and oblivious to the drama that had gone on before he reached the stadium.

Dorando was disqualified for receiving assistance, and the gold medal went to Hayes. But it was the Italian who had captured the hearts of the British public, and Queen Alexandra was so moved by his performance that she presented him with a special gold cup.

From that day on the official distance of the marathon became 26 miles plus 385 yards – the distance from the White City entrance to the Royal Box.

There was another crazy race in those 1908 London Olympics. London-based Scot Wyndham Halswelle became the only man to win an Olympic medal unchallenged. He ran a solo lap in a rerun 400 metres final after his two American rivals had pulled out in protest over the disqualification of their team-mate John Carpenter.

The first running of the race had been declared 'nul and void' after British officials ruled that Carpenter had run across Halswelle and blocked his run to the tape.

Halswelle, a regular soldier who was a lieutenant in the British Army, then went through the farcical motions of running the race as he experienced the loneliness of the short-distance runner.

The dispute had a huge influence on the decision to run future 400-metre races in lanes. Tragically, one-lap hero Halswelle was killed by a sniper's bullet during the First World War.

One of the most famous of all British Olympians shares with me the fact that he used to be a plasterer. I just hope he was better at plastering than he was at ski jumping. I refer, of course, to the one and only Eddie 'The Eagle' Edwards, who became the talk of the 1988 Winter Olympics in Calgary because he was so hopeless at his event.

He had everybody rolling on the floor laughing as his attempts at soaring became stone-like flops to the snowy slope far below. His trademark flapping arms and thick pebble spectacles made him look like Mr Magoo, and he was so unintentionally entertaining that President Reagan used to interrupt meetings at the White House to watch whenever he was on television.

Eddie decided to enter for the Olympics after just a few practice jumps at the dry ski slope in his hometown of Cheltenham. By the time of the Games, he felt ready to challenge the world's top ski jumpers, but he admitted to a serious handicap: his glasses would steam up as he crouched at the top of the jump, and he said he could never see the take-off point.

Everybody took Eddie to their hearts as being representative of the true Olympic spirit, with taking part rather than winning the main aim.

He managed to cause huge amusement on and off the slopes. When he arrived at the airport after his flight from London his bag split open, and fellow passengers were treated to the sight of Eddie running round and round the luggage carousel trying to pick up odd bits of clothing.

When he got to the ski jump for training he found that his equipment had been damaged at the airport, and while it was being repaired he missed two practice jumps and had to make do with just one. After making a safe landing, he returned to his cabin only to find he had been locked out, with his clothes inside.

He then made his way to the press centre, but he did not have the correct pass so was barred from his own press conference!

Few can name who won his event, but stone-last Eddie was famous throughout the world.

When a film of his adventures was being cast, it was suggested that Ewan McGregor should get the title role. 'He's not handsome enough,' Edwards protested. 'It should be Brad Pitt.'

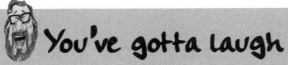

# You've gotta laugh

The middle-aged television executive and his wife of twenty years were lying in bed. He was reading and she was half concentrating on a crossword, with a wandering mind.

'Darling,' she said, looking up from the paper.

'Um?' he replied, engrossed in his book.

'If I died would you get married again?' she asked.

Wondering if this was a trick question, he thought for a moment before answering, 'I don't see why not. Our marriage has been a happy one and you'd want me to be happy again, wouldn't you?'

'Yes, I suppose,' she replied.

They continued in silence for a while, the husband going back to his book and his wife giving floating concentration to her crossword.

'Darling,' she started again.

'Um?' he responded, a little irritated to have his reading interrupted again.

'If you got married again, would you let your new wife wear my dresses?'

He put his book down and gently took her hand. Again realising this was a loaded question with no satisfactory answer, he thought for a moment and said, 'I suppose I would. After all, it would be a shame just to throw away those nice clothes of yours.'

They lapsed back into silence, he returning to his book and she doodling with a pencil on the crossword grid.

'Darling,' she once again started.

'Um?' he replied, wondering what was coming next.

'Would you let her wear my shoes?'

This time he did not even look up from his book as he responded: 'Yes, and for the same reason. It would be a shame to throw away all your expensive shoes.'

They lapsed back into silence, the husband reading and the wife getting into a more depressed mood as she absent-mindedly shaded in the white squares on the crossword.

'Darling,' she said, renewing the inquisition.

'Um?' he replied.

'Would you let her use my new golf clubs?'

Without hesitation, he answered, 'Of course not, she's left-handed.'

# Hark who's talking about sport

**Paul Hogan:**
'Cricket needs brightening up a bit. My idea is that they should *start* with the drinks break, and give the players something with a bit of punch in it. It always works in our picnic matches.'

**Geoffrey Boycott:**
*(questioning the legendary status of W. G. Grace)*
'Unless I'm crackers or something, I've scored a bloody lot more runs than that bearded old bugger.'

**Andrew (Freddie) Flintoff:**
'I enjoy hitting the ball and trying to bowl fast, and that is what I do.'

**Henry Blofeld:**
'It's the sort of simple catch he would have caught ninety-nine times out of a thousand.'

**Richie Benaud:**
'The hallmark of a great captain is to be able to win the toss at the right time.'

**Greg Norman:**
'I owe a lot to my parents – and in particular my mother and father.'

**Darren Gough:**
'You can't have eleven Darren Goughs in your side – it would drive you nuts. It would be like having eleven Phil Tufnells.'

**Lee Trevino:**
'I'm going to win so much on the tour this year that even my caddie will make it into the Top Twenty money-winners list.'

**Jackie Gleason:**
*(on the problems of being an overweight golfer)*
'If I put the ball where I can see it, I can't reach it. If I put the ball where I can reach it, I can't see it.'

**Christy O'Connor:**
'If I wasn't a professional golfer you wouldn't catch me playing the game if they paid me.'

**Bob Charles:**
*(first left-handed winner of the British Open)*
'It's a big advantage to be a left-handed golfer. Nobody knows enough about your swing to be able to mess you up with advice.'

**Doug Sanders:**
'I think those golfers who look as if they got dressed in the dark should be penalised two shots for offending the public eye.'

**Michael Bonallack:**
*(Royal and Ancient secretary)*
'We have no restrictions at the Royal and Ancient except that it's a male club.'

**Hubert Green:**
'Ninety-five per cent of putts that finish short don't go in.'

**Tom Watson:**
'Muirfield without a wind is like a lady undressed. There's no challenge.'

**Sam Snead:**
'I once shot a wild, charging elephant in Africa and it kept coming at me until dropping to the ground at my feet. I wasn't a bit scared. It takes a four-foot putt to scare me to death.'

**Walter Hagen:**
'Never hurry, never worry and be sure to smell the flowers along the way.'

**Muhammad Ali:**
'When you're as great as I am it's hard to be humble.'

**Jake La Motta:**
'I fought Sugar Ray Robinson so many times it's a wonder I didn't get sugar diabetes.'

**Willie Pep:**
*(former world featherweight champion)*
'I had the bravest manager in the world. He didn't care who I fought.'

**Muhammad Ali:**
'Sonny Liston is so ugly that when he cries the tears run down the back of his head.'

**Sonny Liston:**
'I don't think this kid Clay [Ali] is all there. I think he's scrambled in the marbles.'

**Muhammad Ali:**
'Joe Frazier's so ugly his face should be donated to the World Wildlife Fund.'

**Joe Frazier:**
'Let's see what Ali has to say for himself when his big mouth is full of my fist.'

**Joe Bugner:**
'Boxers are only prawns in this game.'

**Chris Eubank:**
*(asked if he had considered writing his autobiography)*
'On what?'

**Bob Hope:**
'In my boxing days they called me Bob "Rembrandt" Hope because I spent so much time on the canvas.'

**Stirling Moss:**
'There are two things a man will never admit doing badly – driving a car and making love.'

**Murray Walker:**
'We now have exactly the same situation as we had at the start of the race, only exactly the opposite.'

**Jimmy White:**
'I don't want to be disrespectful to my fellow snooker players, but it is a joke how I keep losing to so many mugs.'

**Frank Carson:**
'Somebody threw a petrol bomb at Alex Higgins once. He drank it.'

**David Vine**
'Here we are in the Holy Land of Israel – a Mecca for tourists.'

**Fred Perry:**
'John McEnroe needs to sit down and make up his mind where he stands.'

**David Coleman:**
'There goes Juantorena down the back straight, opening his legs and showing his class.'

**José Mourinho:**
'I am in the news every day. I think they really like my overcoat, they really like my haircut, they really like my face, they really like my behaviour, they really like to talk about me.'

**Tiger Woods:**
'The perfect script as far as I am concerned would be playing with my greatest rival while leading by ten. If you're going to dream, let's dream a good one.'

**Sam Torrance:**
'If I thought it would help my game, I would ask Donald Duck for advice.'

**Woody Allen:**
'I was not noticeably good at sports at school. I even failed to make the chess team because of my height.'

# 8  And the Loser is . . .

We do love to pat ourselves on the back in the luvvie land of film, theatre and television. There are now so many awards shows that it's a wonder we have time to fit the making of the films, plays and television programmes around them.

One of the big nights of my life was when I collected the Best Comedy Actor award in 1999 for my performances as Jim Royle, and what made it even more memorable was that Caroline Aherne won Best Comedy Actress, Jessica Stevenson Best Newcomer and *The Royle Family* carried off the Best Sitcom title. It was the finest foursome since England's four goals against West Germany in the 1966 World Cup final.

The British Comedy Awards always guarantee a good laugh, particularly when resident host Jonathan Ross is in full flow. He was on top of his game at the 1993 show, which has gone down in television legend because of the contribution of the outrageous Julian Clary.

Former Chancellor Norman Lamont had made one of the earlier presentations before Clary came on to announce the winner of the Best Entertainment Series, bringing sudden danger to live TV. The set looked as if a deranged Alan Titchmarsh – with greenery and plants everywhere – had designed it. This is, verbatim, what happened when Clary made his entrance:

JONATHAN: Good to see you – how's it hanging?

JULIAN: Oh, very well thank you. Very nice of you to recreate Hampstead Heath for me here (a lot of audience giggling). As a matter of fact, I've just been fisting Norman Lamont ... (explosion of laughter that goes on for a full half minute)

JONATHAN: (visibly panicking) Let me ask you, Julian ... (tails off)

JULIAN: (adding a punchline that was out of the gay club scene) Talk about a red box ...

(a cut away to Richard and Judy in hysterics, and other members of the audience literally crying with laughter)

JONATHAN: (struggling) So, uh ... How did you jump to the front of the queue then?

JULIAN: Just clawed my way through ...

JONATHAN: (talking to the unseen director, with a glazed look on his face) Are we still on?

It was a mesmeric TV moment that has never been shown again, yet has become the benchmark for just how far they dare go with the *Comedy Awards Show* material. They really made a fist of it.

A less outrageous but just as memorable event happened during the 2000 *National TV Awards* at the Royal Albert Hall, when Richard Madeley and his wife Judy Finnegan were on stage receiving an award for Best Daytime Programme. Judy's black dress came undone to give the nation a flash of her cleavage. John Leslie, who was then hosting *This Morning*, came dashing from the stalls to cover Judy's embarrassment. Later, Leslie appeared in the news more for his *undressing* of ladies.

One of the best awards show anecdotes I have stumbled on was not reported, and I only got the full story because a member of the production staff is a pal of mine. Robert Mitchum was the surprise last guest to receive an award on a *TV Times* show for his performance in the series *The Winds of War*.

It was kept top secret that Mitchum had flown in from the United States especially to collect his trophy, and there was a news blackout to stop anybody finding out before the live show.

Mitchum arrived too late for a rehearsal and was shown to the green room, where he proceeded to fill his huge pipe with what one onlooker described as 'the biggest wedge of weed I have ever seen'.

It was a well-known fact that Mitchum had been a regular user of marijuana, and had once served sixty days in prison for possession. (Asked on his release what prison had been like, he said: 'Very pleasant . . . Palm Springs without the riff raff.')

Mitchum sat quietly in the corner of the green room watching the monitor on which the show was being screened, and he seemed to be getting slowly but pleasantly stoned. Either that or jet lag had taken on a new light-headed quality. He was into a relaxed world of his own when the floor manager came to the green room to prepare him for his walk-on in the big surprise climax to the show.

The floor manager positioned Mitchum in the wings of the stage, and told him that his cue was to walk on when show host Bruce Forsyth said: 'And here, flown in especially from the United States . . . Hollywood legend, Robert Mitchum.'

He was still smoking his pipe until a health and safety official insisted that he put it out. Mitchum tucked it into his top pocket, and dreamily watched Bruce going through one of his joke routines with the audience. He listened hard for his name.

Incredibly, superpro Brucie had one of his rare lapses and started to wind up the show without announcing that Mitchum was there. 'Thanks for watching and it was nice to see you, to see you nice . . .' he said.

The purple-faced floor manager was waving his arms like a demented tic-tac man to tell Bruce that there was still the final award to be made to Mitchum, who stood looking blankly and wondering if perhaps he had already been on stage and had come off.

Brucie quickly started ad-libbing his way out of trouble. 'But before we go, one last great surprise,' he said, having already bid goodnight to viewers. 'Flown in especially from the United States . . . Hollywood legend, Robert Mitchum.'

A quick shove in the back by the floor manager sent an almost comatose Mitchum on to the stage. He was given his award and barely mumbled a thank you before the closing titles were up and running.

Just as the commercials were about to run, Mitchum could be heard saying: 'Is that it?'

What a great story to kick off my collection of award show anecdotes, focusing mainly on the big daddy of them all, the Oscars . . .

Samuel L. Jackson is as blunt and upfront a character as you can meet. He was nominated for Best Supporting Actor in *Pulp Fiction*. When he lost to Martin Landau (for his role in Tim Burton's *Ed Wood*), Samuel did not go through the usual pretence of being a good loser. Instead of going down the cliché road of politely clapping his hands, he uttered an audible 'Shit!'

This was picked up by television microphones over a close-up of Samuel looking very pissed off. He explained later, with biting honesty: 'There was no need for me to sit there clapping and saying, "I'm so glad Martin won," because I wasn't. I was disappointed that I didn't win and I expressed that.'

How much more entertaining award shows would become if everybody adopted that attitude. Can you imagine if people suddenly started telling the truth about what they thought of the winning actors and directors? 'She only got the Oscar because she's slept with more Academy members than me.' 'Best director? He couldn't direct traffic in a one-way street.' While on the surface Hollywood is all luvvie-duvvie, that crazy corner of California is actually a hotbed of betrayals and back-stabbing.

To paraphrase Oscar Wilde's famous quote on fox hunting ('the unspeakable in pursuit of the uneatable'), the Oscars represent in most cases the unworthy in pursuit of the unattainable.

But it doesn't stop every actor dreaming of one day sitting out front at the Academy Awards ceremony and hearing their name coming after the magic words: 'And the winner is . . .'

In the immediate post-war years, Bob Hope reigned as the Academy Awards' host, and Johnny Carson succeeded him. In the modern era, Billy Crystal proved himself the new king and has hosted the show eight times. Most people agree that it was in the 1992 show that he surpassed himself. The ceremony was dominated by *The Silence of the Lambs* and Billy made a hilarious entrance strapped to a stretcher and wearing a muzzled mask in the style of Hannibal Lecter.

Other outstanding Crystal moments centred on cleverly editing himself into the nominated films or singing a medley of all their plots. Hosting the 2000 Oscars, he jokingly 'read the minds' of several of the assembled guests. And what did he think the delicious and distinguished Dame Judi Dench was thinking? 'This thong is killing me!'

At the 1992 show, Hal Roach – one of the great Hollywood pioneers who had just celebrated his hundredth birthday – attempted to respond to an Oscar tribute by making an unmiked speech from his seat that nobody could hear. Billy Crystal, thinking brilliantly on his feet, said: 'This is fitting because Mr Roach started in silent films.'

In a year when most of the major awards were going to overseas talent, Crystal quipped: 'Well, the way things are going, aside from wheat and auto parts, America's biggest export is now the Oscar.'

Steve Martin said of hosting the 2001 Oscars: 'This is really like making love to a beautiful woman. Even if you do your best to keep things fresh and exciting for three hours, you're still painfully aware that you will be dumped as soon as a better man comes along. This is only something I get to do when Billy Crystal's out of town.'

In a pee-take of the rash of reality shows, he added: 'Be sure to stay tuned for the whole show because at the end we are going to vote somebody out of show business!'

When the Oscars were first shown in colour on television, host Bob Hope said: 'For the first time, you will be able to see the losers turn green.'

It should have been the most memorable moment of his career for 1982 Best Animated Short Story Oscar-winner Zbigniew

185

Rybczynski. But everything that could go wrong did go wrong in spectacular fashion. First, nobody could get their tongues round his great Scrabble-hand of a name. Presenter Kristy McNichol tried and failed, making a mess of the pronunciation when announcing the nominations, and then declaring: 'And the winner is Zbigniewski Sky . . . Something!'

The Polish director managed to interpret that he had won, and came happily bouncing up on to the stage. With a female interpreter alongside him, he said: 'I made a short film, so I will speak very short . . . I am dreaming that one day I will speak longer from this place.' That was as far as he got.

The orchestra got a signal that his speech was over and drowned out the rest of what he tried to say with the exit music. Co-presenter Matt Dillon tried to guide him off stage, while Rybczynski was attempting to steal a kiss from Kristy McNichol. 'This is a Slavic custom,' the interpreter told the audience. 'We are a very warm people.'

She then tried to deliver the rest of Rybczynski's acceptance speech, which was in praise of Solidarity leader Lech Walesa and the new Poland. The orchestra played louder, and the Oscar-winner and his interpreter were swept off the stage.

It got worse for poor Zbigniew. He stepped outside for a quick smoke, and when he had finished his re-entry to the theatre was barred by a job's-worth security guard. 'But I have Oscar,' the perplexed Pole tried to tell him.

The guard still refused to let him in, and as Zbigniew tried to push past a scuffle broke out during which kicks were exchanged. Other security men came rushing in, and the unfortunate Rybczynski was hustled off to spend a night in the local jail.

Interviewed the next morning by reporters after all charges of assault had been dropped, he said philosophically through his interpreter: 'Success and defeat are quite intertwined.'

In his acceptance speech after receiving the Best Actor Oscar for *Philadelphia*, Tom Hanks said: 'My thanks to Rawley Farnsworth, my high school drama teacher, who taught me, "To act well the part, there all the glory lies" . . . and thanks to my former classmate John Gilkerson, two of the finest gay Americans, two wonderful men that I had the good fortune to be associated with.'

There was the little matter that Rawley Farnsworth had not been 'outed' to his family and friends, who sat gaping at their television sets as Hanks innocently revealed to the world that he was gay. This led to the plot three years later of the movie *In & Out*.

**What a gay day! Tom Hanks accidentally 'outed' his old acting teacher after accepting the Best Actor Oscar for his stunning performance in *Philadelphia*.**

David Niven lived up to his super-cool image when a streaker raced across the stage while he was introducing Elizabeth Taylor at the 1974 Academy Awards. David waited for the nude exhibitionist to complete his run, and then said: 'The only laughs that man will ever get are by stripping off and showing his shortcomings.'

The audience erupted with applause and laughter at this brilliant ad-lib, and Henry Mancini – conducting the orchestra – quickly got them to play 'Sunnyside Up'.

Show director Marty Passetta said later: 'I had a dozen shots of the streaker on my monitors. All I can tell you is that he wasn't Jewish.'

Marty Feldman, pop-eyed British comedian, made a similar gag at the 1976 Oscars when voted Best Supporting Actor for his performance in *Silent Movie*. He closely examined the Oscar statuette and told the audience: 'He's not Jewish.' He then turned the trophy upside down and added: 'What d'you know. It's made in Hong Kong.'

In fact the Academy Awards statuette was designed in 1928 by MGM art director Cedric Gibbons, who doodled it on to a page and then handed it to a sculptor named George Stanley. He was paid five hundred dollars to produce the first batch of Oscars. The design has not changed since, except for the number of holes in the film spool upon which the Oscar figure stands. In 1929, the spool had five holes, which represented the five branches of the Academy; now it has thirteen, for thirteen branches.

It was named affectionately after Academy executive Margaret Herrick said that it resembled her Uncle Oscar.

Elliott Gould and Isabelle Adjani were joint presenters of the Best Film Editing award at the 1976 Oscars. After they had taken turns reading out the nominees, Adjani said: 'And the winner is . . .' Before she could give a name Gould jumped in with: 'Indiana, 86 to 68.' That was the score of the NCAA basketball final being played that night.

In his role as president of the Screen Actors' Guild, Ronald Reagan awarded the Best Picture Oscar at the 1947 Academy Awards. As clips of the nominees rolled, Reagan declared that the footage represented 'the glories of our past, the memories of our present, and the inspiration of our future'.

He could not understand why his carefully scripted words were being greeted with laughter rather than the respectful awe that he thought they deserved.

The future President of the United States was so busy concentrating on his cue cards that he did not realise that because of technical problems the clips of the nominated films were being shown backwards, upside down and on the ceiling!

A broken leg prevented Best Supporting Actress Alice Brady from being present at the 1937 awards show to collect her Oscar. As she was announced as the winner, a smart-looking gentleman came out of the audience and accepted the award on her behalf.

Weeks later Brady informed the Academy that she had still not received her Oscar, and that she had not sent anybody along in her place.

The trophy was never seen again.

The longest acceptance speech after winning an Academy Award was made by Greer Garson when receiving the Best Actress Oscar for *Mrs Miniver* in 1942. She gushed on for what seemed like hours at a time when the entire world was saying, 'Will the war be over by Christmas?' Suddenly they were asking in Hollywood: 'Will this speech be over before the war ends?'

Presenter Joan Fontaine got so bored she returned to her seat while Garson ('I was completely unprepared for this') went on and on and on. She never won another Oscar. Perhaps that made her speechless.

Learning from the mistake Garson had made in going on too long, Jane Wyman (then Mrs Ronald Reagan) made one of the shortest acceptance speeches at the Oscars in 1949. 'I accept this very gratefully for keeping my mouth shut for once,' she said, after her winning performance as a mute character in *Johnny Belinda*. 'I think I'll do it again.' And she sat down.

But this was a marathon speech compared to the one delivered by Welsh-born Ray Milland when he won the Best Actor Oscar in 1946 for his performance in the harrowing *The Lost Weekend*. He accepted the award, bowed theatrically to the audience and walked off without a word.

Geraldine Page gave herself no chance of winning the Best Actress Oscar for her performance in the 1985 film *The Trip to Bountiful*. She was so sure one of the other nominees would be named that she kicked off her shoes and relaxed in her seat watching the show. She could not believe her ears when the announcement came from presenter F. Murray Abraham: 'And the winner is . . . oh, I consider this woman the greatest actress in the English language . . . Geraldine Page!'

The television director called for reaction shots of Geraldine, but the cameraman couldn't find her. She was ducked down below the seats hurriedly putting on her shoes!

Julie Andrews was peeved, to say the least, when, despite her award-winning performances in the stage version, the film role of Eliza Dolittle went to Audrey Hepburn. It was the decision of Warner Bros chief Jack Warner that Hepburn should get the part. *My Fair Lady* captured several Oscars, but Hepburn failed to get the Best Actress trophy. In that year it went to Julie Andrews for her memorable portrayal of Mary Poppins.

Making her acceptance speech, Julie could not resist a stiletto thrust: 'I'd like to thank all those who made this possible . . . particularly Jack Warner.'

How does the song go? 'A spoonful of medicine makes the sugar go down . . .'

Scouse lass Glenda Jackson won Oscars for *Women in Love* (1969) and *A Touch of Class* (1973). In a voice that gave no clue to her Birkenhead roots, she said: 'My mother polishes them to within an inch of their lives until the metal shows. That sums up the Academy Awards – all glitter on the outside and base metal coming through.'

She now prefers to play a supporting role in the House of Commons where there are almost as many actors as in Hollywood.

Iconic director Frank Capra told this Academy Awards story against himself. 'I was a very confident young guy when I first broke into the business,' he said. 'When I directed the comedy *Lady for a Day* I was so certain that I was going to win the Best Director Oscar that I rented a mansion in Beverly Hills, wrote thank-you notes and speeches, sent out invitations for a victory party and bought a new and very expensive tuxedo for the evening.

'When Oscar presenter Will Rogers opened the envelope to announce the winner, he went into a long speech about a young man who had risen from the bottom of the business. That was me OK. Then he said that the winner was somebody who had great talent and total dedication. Yes, it was me. At last he looked out into the audience and said: "He's a great guy and I am proud to call him a friend . . . Come on up and get it, Frank!"

'It was my great moment. I stood triumphantly, acknowledged the applause and made my way to the stage. Imagine my shock when coming down the other aisle was another candidate. Suddenly I realised that I was the wrong Frank. The winner was *Cavalcade* director Frank Lloyd!

'This was the most embarrassing experience of my life and I swore never to go to another Academy Awards ceremony.'

In fact, he was back the following year of 1935 when his film *It Happened One Night* swept the board and became the first movie to take all five major Oscars.

Olivia de Havilland set the record for the most 'thank-yous' in an Oscars night acceptance speech. She managed an individual expression of gratitude to twenty-seven people who had helped her on the way to her Oscar for the 1946 film *To Each His Own*. But this was eclipsed in 1998 when *Titanic* producer Jon Landau managed to thank forty-five people. He had sunk the old record without trace.

Paul Newman was conspicuous by his absence when he won the Best Actor Oscar for his 1987 performance in *The Color of Money*. 'I have been nominated seven times and never ever won,' he said before the show. 'Perhaps by staying away I can become a winner.'

When they were trying to limit Oscar acceptance speeches to a maximum of forty-five seconds, it was suggested it might help if winners name-checked only their current spouses! Here are some of the most memorable Academy Award acceptance speech lines.

Ruth Gordon, winning an Oscar at the age of seventy-two for her role in *Rosemary's Baby*: 'I can't tell you how encouraging a thing like this is.'

Diminutive composer Paul Williams, receiving his Oscar for writing 'Evergreen' with Barbra Streisand: 'I was going to thank all the little people, but then I remembered I *am* the little people.'

When Kevin Spacey returned to his seat after his press conference following his Best Supporting Actor success for *The Usual Suspects* in 1995, he found his mother still in tears. 'Was it something that I said?' he asked her.

Perhaps she was thinking back to when Kevin was a seven-year-old boy. 'I used to come out of the curtains in the kitchen,' he recalled, 'and accept anything my mother wanted to give me as an Oscar and then make a speech.'

Four years later Kevin was back on stage again to receive his Best Actor Oscar for *American Beauty*, and he proved all his speech rehearsals as a kid had been worthwhile. He opened by saying: 'This has definitely been the highlight of my day. I hope it's not all downhill from here.'

Louise Fletcher, Best Supporting Actress for her role as nasty Nurse Ratched in *One Flew Over the Cuckoo's Nest*: 'I've loved being hated by you.' She then thanked Jack Nicholson for making 'being in a mental institution like being in a mental institution'.

Robert De Niro, accepting Best Actor for *Raging Bull* (and, boy, how he deserved it!), thanked the boxer he portrayed – Jake La Motta – 'even though he's suing us'.

Steven Spielberg, for *Schindler's List* in 1994, after years of being passed over by the Academy: 'Oh, wow. This is the best drink of water after the longest drought of my life.'

Dianne Wiest, Best Supporting Actress for *Hannah and Her Sisters*: 'Gee, this isn't like I imagined it would be in the bathtub.'

Cuba Gooding Jr, Best Supporting Actor for *Jerry Maguire*, ran over his allotted time and decided to battle with the drowning music: 'I love you!' he shouted as the music cued. 'Tom Cruise! I love you, brother! I love you, man! . . . Everybody, I love you. I love you all. Cameron Crowe! James L. Brooks! James L. Brooks, I love you. Everybody who's involved with this, I love you. I love you. Everybody involved.'

Laurence Olivier is remembered as one of the greatest actors of all time, but his acceptance speeches could be, well, a little over the top. See what you think. Here in its entirety is his speech for a Lifetime Achievement Oscar that had Hollywood split over whether it was the best or the most boring speech ever made at an awards show. He had been introduced by British-born Hollywood giant Cary Grant:

*Oh, dear friends, how am I supposed to speak after that? Cary, my dear old friend for many a year, from the earliest years of either of us working in this country. Thank you for that beautiful citation and the trouble you have taken to make it and all the warm generosities in it. Mr President, and governors of the Academy, committee members, fellows, my very noble and approved good masters, my colleagues, my friends, my fellow students. In great wealth, the great firmament of your nation's generosities, this particular choice may perhaps be found by future generations as a trifle eccentric, but the mere fact of it – the prodigal, pure human kindness of it – must be seen as a beautiful star in that firmament, which shines upon me; that moment – dazzling me a little, but filling me with the warmth of extraordinary elation, the euphoria that happens to so many of us at the first breath of the majestic glow of a new tomorrow. From the top of this moment, in the solace, in the kindly emotion that is charging my soul and my heart at this moment, I thank you for this great gift, which lends me such a very splendid part of this, your glorious occasion. Thank you.*

Shirley MacLaine went down the classical Olivier route after winning Best Actress for the 1983 film *Terms of Endearment*: 'Films and life are like clay, waiting for us to mould it. And when you trust your own insides and that becomes achievement, it's a kind of principle that seems to me is at work with everyone. God bless that principle. God bless that potential that we all have for making anything possible if we think we deserve it.'

And then she added: 'I deserve this.'

How do the Olivier and MacLaine speeches compare with my main thank-you line when I accepted my Best Comedy Actor award: 'Best comedy actor, my arse!'?

But back to the Oscars . . .

There have been some memorable lines. Rod Steiger thanked the Maharishi. Vanessa Redgrave took a pot shot at the 'Zionist hoodlums'. Screenwriter John Irving acknowledged the Abortion Rights Action League. Michael Moore got a mixed reception for saying, 'Shame on you, Mr Bush. Shame on you.'

Director James Cameron shouted, 'I am the king of the world!' right after requesting a minute's silence for the victims of the real *Titanic*. 'Now let's party until dawn.'

His poorly timed remarks went down like the ship itself.

'You like me, you really like me,' gushed Sally Field in 1985, accepting her second Oscar in five years for *Places in the Heart*.

Sidney Poitier, Best Actor in 1963 for *Lilies of the Field* and the first black man to win that Oscar: 'It has been a long journey to this moment.'

Whoopi Goldberg, Best Supporting Actress for *Ghost*: 'I want to thank everybody who makes movies. As a little kid, you're the people I watched. You're the people who made me want to be an actor. I'm so proud to be here.'

Mickey Rooney, Honorary Oscar: 'When I was nineteen years old I was the number-one star of the world for two years. When I was forty nobody wanted me. I couldn't get a job.'

Cher, Best Actress for *Moonstruck*, caused a stir when she thanked her make-up man, her hairdresser, her assistant . . . and somehow failed to thank her co-stars and her director Norman Jewison.

There was a sharp intake of breath when Jane Fonda was named Best Actress for *Klute* in 1972. Everybody braced themselves for an anti-Vietnam War tirade. 'There's a great deal to say,' she started, 'but I'm not going to say it tonight.' Her father Henry gave a thumbs up. He had implored her not to use the Academy Awards show for yet another rant against the government and the war, a campaign that had earned her the nickname 'Hanoi Jane'.

Catherine Zeta-Jones, aka Mrs Michael Douglas, delivered one of the most emotional speeches when collecting her Oscar for her performance in *Chicago*. Heavily pregnant, she said after a huge gush: 'My hormones are just too way out of control to be dealing with this.'

Six months later she sat down and watched a recording of the presentation. 'I could not recall a thing about it,' she said. 'It was all a blur. I just recall looking down at my swollen ankles and wishing I could knock back a glass of champagne.'

But Catherine was positively laid back and controlled compared with Gwyneth Paltrow, after receiving her Best Actress award for *Shakespeare in Love*. She could barely get the words out between sobs, and her over-the-top speech had everybody cringing on her behalf.

'I want to thank . . . everybody I ever met in my entire life,' said a breathless Maureen Stapleton in 1982, winning Best Supporting Actress for *Reds*. Some years later she was asked what it was like to be remembered as a great actress. 'My dear,' she told the reporter, 'I would have been much more excited being remembered as a great lay.'

How about this for arrogance. Accepting Best Screenplay for *The Philadelphia Story*, Donald Ogden Stewart went on record with the fact that it was he and only he who was responsible for the film's success. The director, producers and actors did not second that opinion.

Jessica Yu, accepting for Best Short Subject Documentary: 'What a thrill. You know you've entered new territory when you realise that your outfit cost more than your film.'

Robin Williams, Best Supporting Actor for *Good Will Hunting*: 'Most of all, I want to thank my father, up there, the man who when I said I wanted to be an actor said, "Wonderful, just have a back-up profession like welding."'

Maurice Jarre, accepting Best Score for *A Passage to India*, the year *Amadeus* won Best Picture: 'I was lucky Mozart was not eligible this year.'

Veteran Jack Palance celebrated his Oscar win for *City Slickers* with an amazing series of one-arm push-ups. When Billy Crystal came on stage Palance brought the house down by repeating the line he had used to Crystal in the film: 'I crap bigger than him.'

Collecting the Best Actor Oscar for his role in *My Left Foot*, Daniel Day-Lewis said: 'You've just provided me with the makings of one hell of a weekend in Dublin.'

Marlon Brando sent Sacheen Littlefeather, in traditional American Indian dress, to accept his Best Actor Oscar for *The Godfather*. She read his words: 'I think awards in this country at this time are inappropriate to be received or given until the condition of the American Indian is drastically altered. If we are not our brother's keeper, at least let us not be his executioner.'

It later transpired that she was not a Native American.

Humphrey Bogart was no great fan of the Oscars. 'To make it fair,' he said, 'everybody should play Hamlet and let the best man win.'

Our highly respected Richard Attenborough, Best Director Oscar-winner for *Gandhi*, challenged even Greer Garson for the longest speech. Try this for size, darlings: 'Gandhi simply asked that we should examine the criteria by which we judge the manner of solving our problems. That surely in the twentieth century, we human beings, searching for our human dignity, could find other ways of ultimately solving our problems than blowing the other man's head off. He begged us to re-examine that criteria . . .'

Jonathan Demme, Best Director for *The Silence of the Lambs*, used the crutch word 'uh' thirty-eight times in a five-minute speech.

Ingrid Bergman summed up what winning an Oscar meant to her: 'My salary doubled, my friends tripled, my kids became more popular at school, the butcher made a pass at me, and my maid asked for a raise.'

When Robert Rich won the Best Screenplay Oscar in 1957 for *The Brave One*, he did not make an appearance. A member of the Writers' Guild received it on his behalf, explaining that Robert was attending the birth of his first child. Nobody in Hollywood had ever met Robert Rich.

The Academy claimed the Oscar back when it was realised that Rich did not exist. Nineteen years later the Oscar was taken out of mothballs and presented to the rightful winner, Dalton Trumbo. He had used 'Robert Rich' as a pseudonym because he had been blacklisted during Senator Joe McCarthy's 'Reds under the bed' witch-hunts.

Roberto Benigni, collecting the first Best Actor Oscar ever awarded for a non-English-speaking part in *La Vita è bella* (*Life Is Beautiful*, 1997) was without doubt the most ecstatic winner. He hurdled over rows of seats and clambered over the bodies of Hollywood stars to get to the stage when his name was announced as the winner.

'I would like to be Jupiter and kidnap everybody and lie down in the ground making love to everybody – because I don't know how to express,' he said, gabbling with excitement. 'It's a question of love. You are really . . . this is a mountain of snow, so delicate, the suavity and the kindness, it is something I cannot forget!'

Benigni's excitement actually peaked backstage. 'I'm so happy', he exclaimed, 'that every organ in my body is moving in a very bad way!'

Meryl Streep, Oscar-winner for *Kramer vs. Kramer* in 1979, got in a panic during the after-show party when she mislaid the trophy. She retraced her steps and found it in the toilet cubicle she had visited earlier in the evening.

Barry Fitzgerald, winner of Best Supporting Actor as Father Fitzgibbon in the 1945 classic *Going My Way*, was practising his golf swing at home and decapitated his Oscar. 'I used a swear word of which Father Fitzgibbon would not have approved,' said the veteran Irish actor.

The Oscars are the most famous of all the awards shows, but there are scores of others that have since come along in almost every category under the sun. There is now even an Awards Awards Show that gives out awards for the best awards shows!

Awards shows, my arse!

The MTV Music Awards are a mega TV event, and they provided one of the biggest laughs when broadcast live from New York's Radio City Music Hall in 2002.

Britney Spears invited Michael Jackson up on stage simply to present him with a giant cake to mark his forty-fourth birthday. She just happened to mention in her introduction that she thought Michael was the artist of the millennium.

Wacko Jacko somehow got it into his head that this meant he was being presented with the Artist of the Millennium award.

'When I was a little boy growing up in Indiana,' he told a star-spangled audience and millions watching on the box, 'if someone had told me I'd be getting the Artist of the Millennium award I'd never have believed it.'

Uh, Jacko, you were not getting it. All you were getting was a cake.

An MTV spokesperson later confirmed: 'There is no such award as the Artist of the Millennium. I think some wires got crossed.'

Jacko was away with the fairies in Never Never Land.

Among those thanked by Jacko before he was ushered off the stage were God, his parents and, for some reason, street magician David Blaine.

Six years earlier, while performing at the Brit Awards, Jacko had been mock-mooned on stage by Pulp singer Jarvis Cocker as a protest at Jackson's pomposity. Jarvis, thank heavens, kept his trousers on!

The Brits are always good for something off the wall, reaching the peak of preposterousness when Sam Fox and Mick Fleetwood gave the little and large show that I mentioned earlier in the book.

Robbie Williams used one of his acceptance speeches to offer to fight Liam Gallagher for a £100,000 stake. Gallagher did not need any lessons from Williams in how to be a young man behaving badly at the Brits. At a previous show he had mimed sticking his award up where the sun does not shine after telling guest presenter Michael Hutchence: 'Has-beens shouldn't be presenting awards to gonna-bes.'

They keep trying to give the Brits extra clout by inviting along politicians, and they usually end up making prats of themselves. Margaret Thatcher never made it on to the guest list, probably because she had previously revealed that her favourite song was 'How Much Is That Doggy in the Window?', but John Prescott got an ice bucket tipped over him by anarchist rocker Danbert Nobacon, and Elton John publicly expressed his disgust when his Outstanding Contribution to Music award was presented to him by Conservative Party chairman Norman Tebbit. This was the same Norman Tebbit who had famously said that no homosexual should hold a position of responsibility.

Fire-eating Russell Crowe brought his own brand of belligerence to the 2002 Bafta Awards. Accepting the Best Actor trophy for his performance in *A Beautiful Mind*, Crowe recited a poem by Irish bard Patrick Kavanagh called 'Sanctity' during his rambling speech. The show went out as a tape-delayed broadcast, and when Crowe watched it later that evening he went ballistic when he discovered the poem had been cut. He sought out one of the show's producers, Malcolm Gerrie, pinned him against a wall and growled: 'You f\*\*\*ing piece of shit. How do you have the audacity to take out the Best Actor's poem? I'll make sure you never work in Hollywood.'

Crowe had the good grace to apologise to Gerrie once he had got his temper under control, but lost it again a week later when the same poem was cut from a speech he made on Australian television.

The poem was actually cut from the Baftas because copyright for it had not been cleared . . . and that's why I am not repeating it here!

The first rule for any awards nominees is that they should be ready to step up to receive their prize when the winner is announced. Actress Christine Lahti was in the ladies' room when her name was called as winner of a Golden Globe in 1998. 'I was just flushing the toilet,' she said later, 'when somebody came dashing into the room shouting, "You've won . . . you've won . . . they're waiting for you."'

By then, Michael J. Fox and Robin Williams on stage had let everybody in the audience know where she was and why they were being kept waiting. Eventually Christine emerged to huge roars, and when she collected her Globe she was (please forgive me) flushed with success.

A year later Christine presented a Globe, deliberately with a sheet of toilet paper stuck to her shoe.

Sports awards shows are massively popular. One of the early ones was on BBC TV *Grandstand*. MCC chairman Gubby Allen was

Don't you hate it when you see trophy winners going over the top when they are named as winners at award ceremonies? Look at this prat kissing his National TV Award. Oh, hold on. It's me! To paraphrase the Olympic ideal, 'It's not the taking part that matters, it's the winning!' This was a trophy I collected on behalf of *The Royle Family* team.

invited on the show to name the Cricketer of the Year. Presenter Frank Bough said: 'And now the big moment, Gubby. Please open the envelope and tell us who has won.'

Gubby reached into his jacket pocket. Nothing. Then in his other pocket. Nothing. His inside pocket. Nothing. Then he announced: 'I've mislaid the envelope.'

'In that case,' said Bough, 'can you please tell us who has won?'

Poor old Gubby had a complete blank, and an embarrassed Bough said: 'Well, these things happen with live television. Let's go to our next event, and when you come back we will, I promise, reveal who is the Cricketer of the Year.'

There have been few wittier men in the world of show business than Frank 'It's the way I tell 'em' Carson. I asked him why Irishmen always answer a question with a question. His response: 'Do we now?'

John Curry, world and Olympic ice-skating champion, was the choice of the Sports Writers' Association as their Sportsman of the Year for 1976. He was guest of honour at the dinner and dance where his trophy was to be presented.

It was staged just before Christmas, and during the evening there was an after-dinner comedy spot featuring ventriloquist Roger De Courcey and his 'companion' Nookie the Bear. While his television act was aimed at a family audience, Roger was very much into adult humour away from the camera.

He told a stream of risqué jokes that made many of those in the audience uncomfortable, and then surpassed himself when Sportsman of the Year John Curry came walking across the empty dance floor after visiting the cloakroom. It was an open secret that John was gay, and his walk was something of a mince.

De Courcey – or was it Nookie? – paused halfway through a joke, stared at Curry making his way towards his seat and said: 'Oh look,

Merry Christmas everybody. Here comes the fairy for the tree.'

There was an embarrassed silence, then some stifled giggles, followed by a roar of protests and booing.

It was the night Nookie the Bear died on his arse.

I will bring down the final curtain on this peep into the world of awards shows by returning to where I started, with the British Comedy Awards. One of the funniest (and rudest) acceptance speeches I ever heard came from the mouth of a former screen wife of mine, the multi-talented actress Kathy Burke. Remember, this was on live television.

Kathy, much more intelligent off stage and screen than some of the characters she plays, is now concentrating on a successful switch to a career as a director.

Awarded Best Comedy Actress for *Gimme Gimme Gimme* at the 2002 British Comedy Awards, she told the audience and millions of viewers watching at home: 'Thank you very much. This is nice . . . and it's about f***ing time. It's a disgrace that *Gimme Gimme Gimme* has won f*** all.'

Kathy then turned her cutting tongue on the critics. She told the 'Groucho Club media mafia': 'I couldn't give a shit about any of you, and what you f***ing think.'

Show host Jonathan Ross said: 'If only they had the courage to put this out live!'

This is the sort of edge the Academy Awards show is missing!

# You've gotta laugh

Two out-of-work Hollywood actors – one a handsome young man in his mid-twenties and the other a beautiful blonde woman – audition for the part of a lion-tamer in a film about a circus.

The director tells them: 'I'm looking for reality, so you really have to learn to tame this lion. I have to warn you that he is ferocious and has eaten three actors so far. Do you still want to audition?'

The actress is desperate for money and agrees to go ahead. The young man feels he cannot lose face, and so says that he will also carry on with the audition.

'Right,' says the director. 'Here's your equipment – a chair, a whip and a gun. Who wants to try out first?'

The woman volunteers. She declines the chair, the whip and the gun and steps right into the lion's cage without anything with which to defend herself. The lion snarls, paws the ground and then starts to charge her. Suddenly she throws open her coat, revealing her beautiful naked body.

The lion stops dead in his tracks, sheepishly crawls up to her and starts licking her ankles. He then licks up her legs, and gradually starts to lick her all over while purring with pleasure.

'That's great,' says the amazed director. 'I've never seen anything like it in my life.'

He then turns to the young man and asks, 'D'you think you can do that?'

'No problem,' replies the actor. 'Just get that f***ing lion out of the way.'

# Hark who's talking wittily

**Noël Coward:**
'I have only one superstition. I will never sleep thirteen to a bed.'

**Oscar Levant:**
'I knew Doris Day before she became a virgin.'

**Groucho Marx:**
'Ever since the public found out that Lassie was a boy, the public have thought the worst of Hollywood.'

**Groucho Marx:**
*(departing words to his party host)*
'I've had a wonderful evening, but this wasn't it!'

**Angus Deayton:**
'When one door closes, another one falls on top of you.'

**Barbara Windsor:**
'They say an actress is only as good as her parts. Well my parts have done me pretty well, darling.'

**Lucille Ball:**
'The secret of staying young is to live honestly, eat slowly, and lie about your age.'

**Zsa Zsa Gabor:**
*(asked how many husbands she had had)*
'You mean besides my own?'

**Jack Lemmon:**
'If you think it's hard to meet new people, try picking up the wrong golf ball.'

**Jack Nicholson:**
'My mother never saw the irony in calling me a son-of-a-bitch.'

**Jack Nicklaus:**
*(asked the secret of knowing his way around a golf course)*
'The holes are numbered.'

**Gyles Brandreth:**
'John Prescott looks like a terrifying mixture of Hannibal Lecter and Terry Scott.'

**Cindy Crawford:**
'Even I don't wake up looking like Cindy Crawford.'

**Jim Carrey:**
'One thing I hope I'll never be is drunk with my own power and anyone who says I am will never work in this town again.'

**Katharine Hepburn:**
'It's a new low for actresses when you have to wonder what is between her ears instead of her legs.'

**Clint Eastwood:**
'There's only one way to make a happy marriage, and as soon as I learn what it is I'll get married.'

**Spike Milligan:**
'A man loses his dog, so he puts an advertisement in the paper. And it says: "Here boy."'

**Barry Humphries:**
'Sex is the most beautiful thing that can take place between a happily married man . . . and his secretary.'

**Billy Connolly:**
'Marriage is a wonderful invention; but then again, so is a bicycle repair kit.'

**Billy Crystal:**
'Women need a reason to have sex; men just need a place.'

**Jack Dee:**
'One of my friends went on a murder weekend . . . now he is doing life for it.'

**Bob Mortimer:**
'Vic, have you farted?'
**Vic Reeves:**
'No.'
**Bob Mortimer:**
'What, never?'

**Quentin Crisp:**
'Never keep up with the Joneses. Drag them down to your level. It's cheaper.'

**Chris Eubank:**
'Not being born to parents who were accountants was probably my biggest mistake.'

**George Burns:**
'I was married by a judge. I should have asked for a jury.'

**Dorothy Parker:**
'If you want to know what God thinks of money, just look at the people he gave it to.'

**Don Rickles:**
*(acid-tongued American comedian)*
'Who picks your clothes – Stevie Wonder?'

**Lana Turner:**
'A successful man is one who makes more money than his wife can spend. A successful woman is one who can find such a man.'

**George Burns:**
'Too bad all the people who know how to run the country are busy driving taxi cabs and cutting hair.'

**Clive James:**
'It is only when they go wrong that machines remind you how powerful they are.'

**Michael Caine:**
*(asked about the hugely criticised* Jaws *sequel in which he appeared)*
'I have never seen it, but by all accounts it's terrible. However, I have seen the house that it built, and it's terrific!'

**Nathan Lane:**
*(star of* The Producers*)*
'We were very poor when I was growing up in New Jersey. I remember one Christmas Eve my father going into the back yard and firing a hand gun. Moments later he came back and told us Santa Claus had committed suicide.'

**Phyllis Diller:**
'Never go to bed mad. Stay up and fight.'

**Les Dawson:**
'I went to my doctor and asked for something for persistent wind. He gave me a kite.'

# 9  Celebrity Trivia Lists

Long before Trivial Pursuit became a worldwide craze, I used to collect little-known facts about anything and everything. I was the boy at the back of the class who, during history lessons, was more interested in how many fingers Anne Boleyn had rather than the dates she was on the throne (myth has it that she had six fingers on one hand, which might explain why Henry VIII had her beheaded . . . too many fingers in the pie).

As I grew older I became addicted to the sort of facts about famous people that bring 'I don't believe it' reactions. For instance, did you know that as well as Leo McKern, Rex Harrison and Peter Falk became famous actors despite taking a one-eyed look at the world? They each had a glass eye.

Then there were Aristotle, Sir Edmund Hillary, Henry Fonda and Sherlock Holmes. All, as I'm sure you knew, were celebrity beekeepers.

And no doubt you also knew that the day John F. Kennedy was assassinated in 1963, two giants of literature also died — Aldous Huxley and C. S. Lewis — and got just paragraphs for their obituaries because all the newspaper space went to the events in Dallas.

From gathering facts and anecdotes like the ones in the previous chapters, the next step was to start making lists. While plastering walls or staring at a cell ceiling, I used to amuse myself by making up lists: Liverpool's best left-footed players, Lonnie Donegan's greatest skiffle songs, Prime Ministers I would not have voted for. You get the idea.

For example, here are ten trivial things you may not have known – and may not want to know – about me . . .

- I am a chronic asthmatic (as is Paula Radcliffe and as was Beethoven).
- I passed my City and Guilds exams (as did gardener Alan Titchmarsh and chef Gary Rhodes).
- I play the banjo (as does Steve Martin and as did Winston Churchill).
- I was in a skiffle group in the 1950s (as were Pete Townshend and Ringo Starr).
- I was a plasterer (as was *Thunderbirds* creator Gerry Anderson).
- I was arrested on a charge of which I believed I was totally innocent (as was England football captain Bobby Moore on the eve of the 1970 World Cup finals).
- I drive a campervan (as does chef Jamie Oliver and as did Harrison Ford).
- I started my acting career as an extra (as did Sean Connery and Gary Cooper).
- I played in goal for amateur football teams (as did Sir David Frost and Pope John Paul II).
- I kept a prison diary while banged up (as did Jeffrey Archer and Oscar Wilde).

So that's the theme for this final chapter in my quest for celebrity facts. All the odd things I have collected and collated have been tidied up and put into categories.

The followings lists add up to total trivia about famous people that I hope you will find not only entertaining but, in many cases, enlightening . . .

# An Actor's Life

## 20 fascinating facts about actors

**James Mason** turned down a co-starring role with Alan Ladd because he objected to the director's demand that he should stand in a trench to make the pint-sized Ladd look taller.

**Sir Ralph Richardson** used to arrive at the theatre on his high-powered motorbike in full leathers – and with his pet parrot, José, perched on his shoulder. José would sit in the dressing-room while Sir Ralph was on stage.

**Cary Grant** was fifty-four when he played the son of actress Jessie Royce in the Hitchcock thriller *North By Northwest*. His 'mother' was eight years younger.

**Sean Connery** was fifty-eight and **Dustin Hoffman** fifty-one when they played father and son in the film *Family Business*. Playing Indiana Jones's father, Connery was only twelve years older than Harrison Ford.

**Andy Garcia** was born a Siamese twin. His twin was the size of a tennis ball and was attached to his shoulder. The twin was surgically removed and died. Garcia still has the scar.

**Johnny Depp** has a morbid fear of clowns since suffering a nightmare about them as a child.

**Mel Blanc**, actor and impressionist who provided the voice for Bugs ('What's up, Doc?') Bunny, was allergic to carrots.

**Keanu Reeves** was born in the Lebanon, with an American father and an English mother. His name means 'Cool breeze over the mountains' in Hawaiian. His paternal grandfather was born in Hawaii and his paternal grandmother was of Chinese descent.

**Jamie Farr**, who as Corporal Klinger kept trying to get a discharge by dressing up as a woman in the long-running Korean War comedy *M\*A\*S\*H*, was the only member of the cast who had served as a soldier in the Korean War.

**Roy Rogers**, 'King of the Cowboys', was not allowed to kiss his real-life wife Dale Evans on screen because of strict moral codes. But there was no objection to him kissing Trigger, his famous white horse. Trigger, Dale's horse Buttermilk and their dog Bullet were all stuffed and are now on show in the Roy Rogers Museum in Missouri.

**Pierce Brosnan** owns the typewriter that James Bond creator Ian Fleming used to write his novels. He bought the gold-plated Royal machine at auction in 1994 for £52,800.

**James Dean** melted a million hearts with his smile, but it came through false teeth. He had his front teeth knocked out at school, and wore false ones for the rest of his life. The false teeth and his glasses – he had dodgy eyesight – are on view at the James Dean Memorial Gallery in his home state of Indiana.

**Peter Sellers** was paid a then astronomical £25,000 to provide the voices for the chimps in the first PG Tips commercial, screened in 1956.

**Humphrey Bogart**'s coffin contains a small gold whistle, placed there by his wife Lauren Bacall to mark her memorable line to him in *To Have and Have Not*: 'You know how to whistle, don't you, Steve? You just put your lips together and blow.'

**Yul Brynner** said in many interviews that he was a half-Swiss, half-Japanese named Taidje Khan, born in 1925 on the island of Sakhalin. In reality he was the son of Boris Brynner, a Swiss-Mongolian engineer and inventor, and Marousia Blagovidova, the daughter of a Russian doctor. He was born in Vladivostok in 1915. All of this only came to light five years after his death when his son wrote a biography revealing the man behind the myths.

**Paul Newman** has the most famous blue eyes in cinema history . . . but while serving in the US Navy he failed a trial as a pilot because he is colour-blind.

**John Travolta** has inadvertently had an enormous impact on **Richard Gere**'s career. Travolta turned down the leads for *Days of Heaven*, *American Gigolo*, *An Officer and a Gentleman* and *Chicago*. Gere took the parts, and won acclaim for each performance.

**Mike Myers** is the Canadian-born son of a former British Army cook. His mum and dad are both Scousers, and Mike grew up speaking with a Liverpudlian accent.

**Charlie Chaplin** once entered a Charlie Chaplin lookalike contest, and finished third.

**Danny DeVito** had just conquered a chain-smoking addiction and kicked the habit when he landed a role in *The War of the Roses* that called for heavy smoking. Throughout the film he smoked cigarettes filled with lettuce.

## What actors did before they were famous

**Humphrey Bogart**, stage manager
**George Clooney**, door-to-door insurance salesman
**Russell Crowe**, bingo caller
**Tom Cruise**, busboy, apartment-block porter, studied for the priesthood
**Cameron Diaz**, model
**Clark Gable**, worked in a tyre factory
**Michael Gambon**, apprentice toolmaker
**John Goodman**, bar-room bouncer
**Hugh Grant**, advertising account executive
**Tom Hanks**, bellboy at a Hilton Hotel
**Dustin Hoffman**, medical student
**Harvey Keitel**, US Marine
**Ewan McGregor**, stableboy
**Liam Neeson**, worked at the Guinness Brewery
**Robert Redford**, art student and stage set designer
**Julia Roberts**, served in a boutique and modelled

## 20 Film stars who started out as extras

**George Clooney**
**Gary Cooper**
**Matt Damon**
**Marlene Dietrich**
**Morgan Freeman**
**Clark Gable**
**Janet Gaynor**
**Paulette Goddard**
**Stewart Granger**
**Jean Harlow**
**David Janssen**
**Harold Lloyd**
**Sophia Loren**
**Patrick Macnee**
**Marilyn Monroe**
**Roger Moore**
**David Niven**
**Rudolph Valentino**
**Michael Wilding**
**Loretta Young**

## 10 Film stars who have played the opposite sex

**Julie Andrews** *(Victor/Victoria)*
**Michael Caine** *(Dressed to Kill)*
**Tony Curtis** *(Some Like It Hot)*
**Alec Guinness** *(Kind Hearts and Coronets)*
**Dustin Hoffman** *(Tootsie)*
**Linda Hunt** *(The Year of Living Dangerously)*
**Jack Lemmon** *(Some Like It Hot)*
**Anthony Perkins** *(Psycho)*
**Barbra Streisand** *(Yentl)*
**Robin Williams** *(Mrs Doubtfire)*

## 10 Film stars who turned down plum roles

**Sean Connery** said 'no' to the lead role in the original *Thomas Crown Affair* (Steve McQueen said 'yes').

**Humphrey Bogart** said 'no' to the lead role in the original *A Star Is Born* (James Mason said 'yes').

Robert Redford turned down the role of *The Graduate* when he was much younger. Enter stage right for his first major role Dustin Hoffman, who graduated to mega-stardom.

**Robert Redford** said 'no' to the lead role in *The Graduate* (Dustin Hoffman said 'yes').

**Cary Grant** said 'no' to the lead role in *The Third Man* (Joseph Cotten said 'yes').

**Vanessa Redgrave** said 'no' to the lead role in *Georgy Girl* (her sister Lynn said 'yes').

**Rod Steiger** said 'no' to the lead role in *Patton: Lust for Glory* (George C. Scott said 'yes').

**Joan Crawford** said 'no' to a leading role in *From Here to Eternity* (Deborah Kerr said 'yes').

**George Raft** said 'no' to the lead role in *The Maltese Falcon* (Humphrey Bogart said 'yes').

**Anthony Newley** said 'no' to the lead role in the original *Alfie* (Michael Caine said 'yes').

**George Segal** said 'no' to the lead role in *10* (Dudley Moore said 'yes').

## 20 Venomous Hollywood put-downs

**Dean Martin** on Hollywood legend **James Stewart**: 'They've erected a statue to Jimmy Stewart, and the statue talks better than he did.'

**Christopher Plummer** on *Sound of Music* co-star **Julie Andrews**: 'Working with her is like being hit over the head with a Valentine's Day card.'

**Rex Reed** on **Marlon Brando**: 'Most of the time he sounds like he has a mouth full of wet toilet paper.'

**Laurence Harvey** on French model turned actress **Capucine** during the filming of *Walk on the Wild Side*: 'Kissing her is like kissing the side of a beer bottle.'

**Clara Bow** on co-starring with **Gary Cooper**: 'When he puts his arms around me, I feel like a horse.'

**Bette Davis** on **Joan Crawford**: 'The best time I ever had with her was when I pushed her down the stairs in *Whatever Happened to Baby Jane?*'

**Jeanne Moreau** on working with **Burt Lancaster**: 'Before he can pick up an ashtray he discusses his motivation for an hour or two. You want to say, "Just pick up the damn ashtray, and shut up!"'

**Louis B. Mayer** on the shapely **Ava Gardner**'s screen test: 'She can't talk. She can't act. She's terrific!'

**Elliot Gould** on meeting his childhood hero **Jerry Lewis**: 'One of the most hostile, unpleasant guys I've ever seen . . . an arrogant, sour, ceremonial, piously chauvinistic egomaniac.'

**Jerry Lewis** on criticism of him: 'People hate me because I am a multi-faceted, talented, wealthy, internationally famous genius.'

**George S. Kaufmann** on **Raymond Massey**'s perfectionist performance as Abraham Lincoln: 'Massey will not be wholly satisfied until he has been assassinated.'

**Sophia Loren** on her Italian screen glamour rival **Gina Lollobrigida**: 'Her personality is limited. She is good as a peasant, but incapable of playing a lady.'

**Gina Lollobrigida** on her Italian screen glamour rival **Sophia Loren**: 'Sophia is a very pretty girl, but she cannot threaten me because she is incapable of playing my roles.'

**Laurence Olivier** on **Marilyn Monroe**: 'She is a professional amateur.'

**Gloria Grahame** on **Ronald Reagan** in his acting days: 'I can't stand the sight of the man. I'd like to stick my Oscar up his ass.'

**Frank Sinatra** on **Robert Redford**: 'Well, at least he has found his true love – what a pity he can't marry himself.'

**Marlon Brando** on **Frank Sinatra**: 'He's the kind of guy that, when he dies, he's going to go up to heaven and give God a bad time for making him bald.'

**Walter Matthau** on his *Hello Dolly!* co-star **Barbra Streisand**: 'I have more talent in my smallest fart than she has in her entire body.'

**Gloria Swanson** on **Lana Turner**: 'She is not even an actress . . . only a trollop.'

**Herman Mankiewicz** on **Orson Welles**: 'There but for the grace of God, goes God.'

# The Name Game

## 20 Nicknames of famous people that stuck

**Buffalo Bill**, William Cody
**The Desert Fox**, Erwin Rommel
**The Pelvis**, Elvis Presley
**Little Sparrow**, Edith Piaf
**The Waltz King**, Johann Strauss
**The Virgin Queen**, Elizabeth I
**The Lone Eagle**, Charles Lindbergh
**Twiggy**, Lesley Hornby
**The Iron Duke**, Duke of Wellington
**The Iron Lady**, Margaret Thatcher
**The Elephant Man**, Joseph Merrick
**The Great Communicator**, Ronald Reagan
**Tricky Dicky**, Richard Nixon
**Superbrat**, John McEnroe
**Calamity Jane**, Martha Jane Canary
**Satchmo**, Louis Armstrong (short for Satchelmouth)
**Bird**, Charlie Parker
**Old Blue Eyes**, Frank Sinatra
**The Red Baron**, Manfred von Richthofen
**Old Blood and Guts**, General George Patton

## 20 People famous enough to be recognised by one name

**Björk**
**Bono**
**Caruso**
**Cher**
**Elvis**
**Eminem**
**Eusebio**
**Gandhi**
**Houdini**
**Jordan**
**Liberace**
**Lulu**
**Madonna**
**Maradona**

Meatloaf
Pavarotti
Pelé
Prince
Seinfeld
Sting

## Original names of 20 actors

Fred Astaire, **Frederick Austerlitz**
Nicolas Cage, **Nicholas Coppola**
Michael Caine, **Maurice Micklewhite**
Michael Crawford, **Michael Dumble-Smith**
Tony Curtis, **Bernie Schwarz**
Kirk Douglas, **Issur Danielovitch Demsky**
Cary Grant, **Archibald Leach**
Laurence Harvey, **Larushka Mischa Skikne**
Rock Hudson, **Roy Scherer**
Boris Karloff, **William Pratt**
Ben Kingsley, **Krishna Bhanji**
Jerry Lewis, **Joseph Levitch**
Herbert Lom, **Herbert Kuchacewich ze Schluderpacheru**
Peter Lorre, **Laszlo Lowenstein**
Dean Martin, **Dino Crocetti**
Jack Palance, **Vladimir Palanuik**
Edward G. Robinson, **Emanuel Goldenberg**
Martin Sheen, **Ramon Estevez**
Robert Taylor, **Spangler Arlington Brugh**
John Wayne, **Marion Morrison**

## Original names of 20 actresses

Anne Bancroft, **Anna-Maria Italiano**
Dyan Cannon, **Samile Diane Friesen**
Cyd Charisse, **Tula Finklea**
Cher, **Cherilyn Sarkisian LaPiere**
Claudette Colbert, **Lily Chauchion**
Joan Crawford, **Lucille Le Sueur**
Yvonne de Carlo, **Peggy Middleton**
Diana Dors, **Diana Fluck**
Greta Garbo, **Greta Gustafsson**

# Acknowledgements

It is with all the sincerity I can muster that I thank the Little, Brown team, and in particular Antonia Hodgson, for their expert help in getting this book out of my head and on to the shelves. I am indebted to Ian Allen, Mike Harkin and Michael Giller for their safety-net checking work on the hundreds of anecdotes that have been knitted together to make Celebrities My Arse! the most complete compilation of funny celebrity stories ever! I am indebted to This Is Your Life past-master Ian Brown and omniscient Richard 'The Snork' Woollen for help on the research front, and we gratefully acknowledge the following websites as being first-class points of reference: www.anecdotage.com, www.IMDb.com, www.en.wikipedia.org, www.celebritywonder.com and www.brainyquote.com.

Thanks to Peter Cotton for a perfectly tailored jacket, to Tamsyn Berryman and Philip Parr for their editorial support, and to Liz Parsons at Empics for help on picture research. Most of all, thanks to all my pals in and around the worlds of television, show business, films and sport who have so willingly helped me dig out the stories. You are too many to mention, but you know who you are! And, of course, thanks to my good pal Norman Giller, for his diligent guidance, and to Rita for being there. I suppose I have also got to thank (this is sounding like an Oscar acceptance speech) Jim Royle for his foreword, but as he is charging me an arm and a leg why the bloody hell should I? His creators, Caroline Aherne and Craig Cash, get the biggest thanks. Without them, Jim Royle would be speechless.

Cheers, the laugh's been on me.

Whoopi Goldberg, **Caryn Elaine Johnson**
Jean Harlow, **Harlean Carpentier**
Susan Haywood, **Edithe Marrener**
Rita Hayworth, **Margarita Carmen Cansino**
Marilyn Monroe, **Norma Jean Baker**
Demi Moore, **Demetria Guynes**
Mary Pickford, **Gladys Smith**
Winona Ryder, **Winona Laura Horowitz**
Raquel Welch, **Raquel Tejada**
Shelley Winters, **Shirley Schrift**
Jane Wyman, **Sarah Jane Falks**

## Original names of 20 singers

Cilla Black, **Priscilla White**
Bono, **Paul Hewson**
David Bowie, **David Jones**
Chubby Checker, **Ernie Evans**
Alice Cooper, **Vincent Furnier**
Elvis Costello, **Declan MacManus**
Doris Day, **Doris Van Kappellof**
Bob Dylan, **Robert Allen Zimmerman**
Judy Garland, **Frances Ethel Gumm**
Crystal Gayle, **Brenda Webb**
Boy George, **George O'Dowd**
Billie Holiday, **Eleanora Fagan**
Englebert Humperdinck, **Arnold Dorsey**
Elton John, **Reg Dwight**
Freddie Mercury, **Faroukh Bulsara**
George Michael, **Georgios Kyriacos Panaylotou**
Cliff Richard, **Harry Webb**
Ringo Starr, **Richard Starkey**
Sting, **Gordon Sumner**
Donna Summer, **LaDonna Andrea Gaines**

## Original names of 20 famous people *(including pseudonyms)*

Woody Allen, **Allen Stewart Konigsberg**
Mel Brooks, **Melvin Kaminsky**
Truman Capote, **Truman Streckfus Persons**

Lewis Carroll, **Charles Lutwidge Dodgson**
David Copperfield, **David Kotkin**
George Eliot, **Mary Ann Evans**
Margot Fonteyn, **Margaret Hookham**
Gerald Ford, **Leslie Lynch King Jr**
Ryan Giggs, **Ryan Green**
Hulk Hogan, **Terry Jean Bollette**
Harry Houdini, **Ehrich Weiss**
Danny Kaye, **David Kaminski**
T. E. Lawrence, **T. E. Shaw**
Lenin, **Vladimir Ilyich Ulyanov**
Joe Louis, **Joseph Barrow**
George Orwell, **Eric Blair**
Vic Reeves, **James Moir**
Sugar Ray Robinson, **Walker Smith**
Roy Rogers, **Leonard Slye**
Mark Twain, **Samuel Langhorne Clemens**

## 20 Famous people who gave their names to inventions

**Biro ballpoint pen** – Laszlo Biro
**Bowie knife** – Jim Bowie
**Braille** – Louis Braille
**Browning firearms** – John Browning
**Bunsen burner** – Robert Bunsen
**Colt revolver** – Samuel Colt
**Davy lamp** – Sir Humphry Davy
**Diesel engine** – Rudolf Diesel
**Dolby noise reduction system** – Ray Dolby
**Gatling Gun** – Richard J. Gatling
**Gillette safety razor** – King Gillette
**Macintosh waterproof coat** – Charles Macintosh
**Mae West inflatable life jacket** – Mae West
**Morse code** – Samuel Morse
**Pasteurisation** – Louis Pasteur
**Richter scale** – Charles Richter
**Saxophone** – Adolphe Sax
**Sousaphone** – John Philip Sousa
**Wellington boot** – Duke of Wellington
**Zeppelin** – Ferdinand von Zeppelin

# Kings, Queens and Presidents

## 10 Amazing facts about royalty

**George I** could not speak English. His language was German. He was fifty-second in line to the throne but the first Protestant on the list. The fifty-one Catholics with greater claims were all ignored.

It took **Louis XVI** of France and Marie Antoinette seven years to consummate their marriage.

**Henry VIII** picked out Anne of Cleves as his fourth wife from a selection of flattering portraits by court painter Hans Holbein. It was like a very early edition of *Blind Date*. When Henry met Anne for the first time he compared her to a horse – 'she hath the face of a Flanders mare'. The marriage was not consummated and was annulled after just six months.

When **Emperor Leopold II** of Belgium married Marie Henrietta he was too ill to attend the wedding, so his brother Archduke Charles took the vows on his behalf.

At his maddest, **George III** insisted on saying the word 'peacock' at the end of every sentence. Once, at the Opening of Parliament, he started his address to the House: 'My Lords and Peacocks . . .'

**Richard II** made pub signs compulsory in 1393 (Royal Oak, King's Head, Crown and Anchor, etc.) because they served as signposts for travellers. They had to be illustrated for those who could not read.

When he was Prince of Wales, **King George IV** ran up gambling and spending debts of £650,000, roughly the equivalent of £60 million today!

On his way home from the Crusades, **Richard the Lionheart** was kidnapped by Duke Leopold of Austria, who demanded and received £70,000 for his release.

As a naval cadet, Prince George – later **George VI** – passed out bottom of his class. He also had a stammer brought on by fear of his father.

**Queen Victoria** was the target of seven known assassination attempts during her sixty-four-year reign.

### 10 Amazing facts about US Presidents

**George Washington** had false teeth that were made of wood.

**Abraham Lincoln** had the biggest feet in the White House . . . he wore a size 14 shoe. He was also the tallest at six feet, four inches.

**Andrew Jackson** once killed a man in a duel after his adversary had made insulting remarks about his wife and future First Lady, Rachel.

**Thomas Jefferson** wrote his own eulogy, neglecting to mention the fact that he had served as President of the United States.

**Theodore Roosevelt** shook hands with 8,513 people in one day during a gathering at the White House on 1 January 1907.

**James Garfield** could write in Greek with one hand and in Latin with the other at the same time.

**John F. Kennedy** won a medal for gallantry in the same summer of 1944 that his older brother Joseph was killed while on a flying mission in Europe. (Joseph would have got his father's financial support for a presidential campaign had he lived.)

**Jimmy Carter** had a speed-reading rate of 2,000 words per minute, and a far above average comprehension of 95 per cent.

**George W. Bush** is a thirteenth cousin twice-removed of Queen Elizabeth II.

**Bill Clinton** was, in March 1993, the first President to send an e-mail message. (It was *not* to 'that woman' Monica Lewinsky.)

# This Sporting Life

## 20 Sportsmen who got close to perfection

**Lance Armstrong** (USA) Won the Tour de France a magnificent seven times in a row, and beat cancer on the way!

**Björn Borg** (Sweden) A Wimbledon winner in five successive years and French champion a record six times, the 'Ice Borg' Swede completely dominated tennis during his peak years. Pete Sampras won Wimbledon seven times, but without capturing the public imagination, while Roger Federer is looking set to beat all records.

**Don Bradman** (Australia) 'The Don' scored 6,996 runs at an average 99.94 in 52 Tests, despite losing his peak years to the Second World War.

**Joe Davis** (England) Unbeaten at the snooker table from 1926 to 1955, and world champion fifteen times. First man to score an official maximum 147, and the only player to hold the world snooker and billiards titles simultaneously.

**Herb Elliott** (Australia) Runaway winner of the 1500 metres at the 1960 Olympics – twenty metres ahead at the tape. He was never beaten over a mile or 1500 metres.

**Juan Manuel Fangio** (Argentina) Motoring ace who won 24 of his 51 Grand Prix races and was Formula One world champion five times between 1951 and 1957 (and runner-up twice).

**Michael Jordan** (USA) Legendary basketball player with the Chicago Bulls who seemed almost to fly around the court. His many titles included two Olympic gold medals.

**Jim Laker** (England) The Surrey off-spinner's 19 wickets for 90 runs for England against Australia in the 1956 Old Trafford Test remains the nearest to a perfect bowling performance ever witnessed.

**Rod Laver** (Australia) The Rockhampton Rocket is the only tennis player to have won the Grand Slam twice, first as an amateur in 1962 and then as a professional in 1969.

**Carl Lewis** (USA) Won nine Olympic gold medals in total, and emulated Jesse Owens' feat of four golds in one Games at Los Angeles in 1984.

**Rocky Marciano** (USA) The only world heavyweight champion to retire undefeated: forty-nine fights, forty-nine victories. The Brockton Blockbuster also never ducked an opponent.

**Jack Nicklaus** (USA) The Golden Bear of golf won a record twenty Major titles, including his two US Amateur Championships. Tiger Woods is on his tail, but he has yet to knock Jack off his pedestal as the greatest golfer of them all.

**Jesse Owens** (USA) Touched perfection with four gold medals (100 and 200 metres, long jump and sprint relay) in the 1936 Berlin Olympics and silenced Hitler.

**Pelé** (Brazil) Scorer of 1,281 goals in 1,363 first-class football matches, including 97 in 111 internationals. A World Cup-winner with Brazil in 1958, 1962 and 1970.

Jack Nicklaus, the Golden Bear. He touched perfection on the golf course, and always represented his sport with dignity, sportsmanship and charm. Footballers, please take note!

**Lester Piggott** (England) The Classics master, he rode a record thirty Classic winners, including nine in the Epsom Derby. Was first past the post 5,300 times worldwide.

**Steve Redgrave** (England) Five successive Olympic rowing gold medals over a span of sixteen years, a remarkable feat that earned him a knighthood.

**Gordon Richards** (England) Champion Jockey a record 26 times, he rode a then record 4,870 winners and was knighted after winning his one and only Derby in 1953.

**Michael Schumacher** (Germany) Statistically the greatest motor-racing driver of all time. He has most Formula One victories, most pole positions and a record seven world championships.

**Mark Spitz** (USA) Seven gold medals for swimming in the 1972 Munich Olympics, all won in world record times. Absolute perfection.

**Emil Zatopek** (Czechoslovakia) The 'Bouncing Czech' who in the 1952 Olympic Games finished first in the 5000 metres, 10,000 metres and marathon – with the last being his debut at the distance.

## A team of England football captains (*number of times they have skippered England in brackets*)

1.  **Peter Shilton** (15)
2.  **Jimmy Armfield** (15)
3.  **George Hardwick** (13)
4.  **Bryan Robson** (65)
5.  **Billy Wright** (90)
6.  **Bobby Moore** (90)
7.  **David Beckham** (58)
8.  **Kevin Keegan** (31)
9.  **Alan Shearer** (34)
10. **Johnny Haynes** (22)
11. **Gary Lineker** (18)

## 10 England cricket captains who were not born in England

**Gubby Allen** (Middlesex) Born Sydney, Australia, 13 July 1902
**Freddie Brown** (Surrey & Northants) Born Lima, Peru, 16 December 1910
**Colin Cowdrey** (Kent) Born Bangalore, India, 24 December 1932
**Mike Denness** (Kent & Essex) Born Belshill, Lanarkshire, Scotland, 1 December 1940
**Ted Dexter** (Sussex) Born Milan, Italy, 15 May 1935
**Tony Greig** (Sussex) Born Queenstown, South Africa, 6 October 1946
**Nasser Hussain** (Essex) Born Madras, India, 28 March, 1968
**Allan Lamb** (Northants) Born Cape Province, South Africa, 10 June 1954
**Tony Lewis** (Glamorgan) Born Swansea, Wales, 6 July 1938
**Plum Warner** (Middlesex) Born Port of Spain, Trinidad, 2 October 1873

## 10 Cricketers who played Test matches wearing glasses

**Eddie Barlow** (South Africa)
**Bill Bowes** (England)
**Geoff Boycott** (England)
**Clive Lloyd** (West Indies)
**Roy Marshall** (West Indies)

**Mike Smith** (England)
**David Steele** (England)
**Tufty Mann** (South Africa)
**Alf Valentine** (West Indies)
**Zaheer Abbas** (Pakistan)

## 20 Sporting nicknames that stuck

**The Greatest**, Muhammad Ali
**Bites Yer Legs**, Norman Hunter
**The Giraffe**, Jack Charlton
**Brockton Blockbuster**, Rocky Marciano
**The Typhoon**, Frank Tyson
**Master Blaster**, Viv Richards
**Ambling Alp**, Primo Carnera
**Manassa Mauler**, Jack Dempsey
**Brown Bomber**, Joe Louis
**Old Stoneface**, Sonny Liston
**Hurricane**, Alex Higgins
**Toothless Tiger**, Nobby Stiles
**The Master**, Sir Jack Hobbs
**The Thorpedo**, Ian Thorpe
**Golden Bear**, Jack Nicklaus
**Great White Shark**, Greg Norman
**The Galloping Major**, Ferenc Puskas
**The Ghost with a Hammer in his Hand**, Jimmy Wilde
**Whispering Death**, Michael Holding
**Wizard of Dribble**, Sir Stanley Matthews

## 10 Sportsmen who have featured in film biopics

**Muhammad Ali** (*Ali*)
**James J. Braddock** (*Cinderella Man*)
**Bob Champion** (*Champion*)
**James J. Corbett** (*Gentleman Jim*)
**Rocky Graziano** (*Somebody Up There Likes Me*)
**Ben Hogan** (*Follow the Sun*)
**Eric Liddell** (*Chariots of Fire*)
**Jake La Motta** (*Raging Bull*)
**Babe Ruth** (*The Babe Ruth Story*)
**Jim Thorpe** (*Man of Bronze*)

## A team of celebrities who wanted to be footballers

**Ronnie Corbett** was a schoolboy triallist with his local club, Hearts, for whom his cousin was a first-team player.

**David Essex**, as David Cook, was a schoolboy on West Ham's books and was in the same squad as Trevor Brooking.

**Sir David Frost** was an accomplished goalkeeper and Nottingham Forest were at one time interested in signing him.

**Sir Elton John** wanted to follow his cousin, Roy Dwight of Nottingham Forest, into professional football but stuck with the piano.

**Eddie Large** was on Manchester City's books but his dreams died when, aged seventeen, he was knocked down by a bus outside the Maine Road ground.

**Des O'Connor** was courted by Northampton Town but he chose instead to become a Butlin's Redcoat.

**Luciano Pavarotti**, the world's greatest opera tenor, was a promising forward with Modena but he selected singing ahead of soccer.

**Rod Stewart** was an apprentice at Brentford, with an ambition to score the winning goal for Scotland against England at Wembley.

**Jimmy Tarbuck** had two trials at Anfield before going into show business full time, and he remains an avid Liverpool supporter.

**Bradley Walsh** was a young professional on the books of Brentford.

**Mike Yarwood** had a trial as a winger with Oldham Athletic but was told to come back when he had put on some more weight.

*Substitute:*

**Julio Iglesias** was a top-flight goalkeeper who played for Real Madrid reserves before scoring worldwide success as a singer.

# Total Celebrity Trivia

## 20 Famous insomniacs

**Tallulah Bankhead** 'rented' homosexuals to sit at her bedside and stroke her hands until she dropped off to sleep.

**Napoleon Bonaparte** disciplined himself to make do with an average of four hours' sleep a night.

**Winston Churchill** had twin beds, using one in which to toss and turn before switching to the other for what he hoped would be restful sleep.

**Charles Dickens** could not get to sleep unless his bed was facing due north.

**Marlene Dietrich** would have a midnight feast of sardine and onion sandwiches because she found they helped her sleep.

**Alexandre Dumas** walked himself to tiredness with middle-of-the-night strolls while thinking of his next chapter.

**Thomas Edison** catnapped during the day to make up for lost sleep.

**W. C. Fields** had a barber's shop chair placed in his bedroom, because he found stretching out on it induced drowsiness.

**Judy Garland** suffered torture every night and she popped pills to try to find the release of sleep.

**Cary Grant** would watch old movies through the night on television.

**Rudyard Kipling** wrote, 'Pity us! Oh pity us! We wakeful!' during one sleepless night.

**Groucho Marx** stopped sleeping after losing a fortune in the 1929 Wall Street Crash. He used to wake up friends with middle-of-the-night calls and say: 'Can you sleep?'

**Marilyn Monroe** tried the sleeping-pill route, which led to addiction but not satisfactory sleep.

**Bobby Moore** used to go for middle-of-the night walks to try to tire himself out. During an England tour to Russia he was found fast asleep on a Moscow park bench!

**Wolfgang Amadeus Mozart** would lie in bed thinking of his next composition, but it did not lull him to sleep.

**Isaac Newton** often used to work through the night, forgetting that he should have been in bed.

**Theodore Roosevelt** took a shot of brandy in a glass of milk in a bid to induce sleep.

**Earl of Rosebery** gave up the job of Prime Minister because it affected his sleep, and he later wrote in his diaries: 'It is a harrowing experience that no man with conscience would wish upon another.'

**Mark Twain** was once so irritable at his failure to sleep that he threw a pillow at his bedroom window, and there was a crash of breaking glass. The *Huckleberry Finn* author awoke in the morning to find he had missed the window and hit the mirror on his dressing-room table.

**Vincent van Gogh** covered his pillow and mattress with camphor to try to knock himself out.

## 10 Dead celebrities who still rake in a fortune

**Elvis Presley** *Died 16 August 1977* Earns millions of dollars through re-release of records and visitors to his old home at Gracelands.

**Charles M. Schulz** *Died 12 February 2000* The creator of the timeless *Peanuts* cartoons that continue to appear in more than two thousand newspapers and magazines worldwide.

**Frank Sinatra** *Died 15 May 1998* His cleverly produced high-tech show is packing theatres on both sides of the Atlantic, and his records are still massive sellers.

**J. R. R. Tolkien** *Died 2 September 1973* Author of the *Lord of the Rings* series that continues to sell in written form and take billions at the cinema box office.

**John Lennon** *Died 8 December 1980* His remastered solo classics are huge hits, and global sales of records by The Beatles remain consistently high.

**Marilyn Monroe** *Died 5 August 1962* Even more than forty years after her death, her name is in demand for advertising and commercial exploitation. She willed everything to her acting coach Lee Strasberg.

**George Harrison** *29 November 2001* Royalties for his solo compositions ('Something', 'My Sweet Lord') still pour in and there is an ongoing share of the income from The Beatles' catalogue.

**Irving Berlin** *Died 22 September 1989* Legendary songwriter who produced scores of hits during his hundred years on this mortal coil, and the royalties still come rolling in.

**Richard Rodgers** *Died 30 December 1979* He had long-playing partner-

ships with first Lorenz Hart and then Oscar Hammerstein, and composed the music for such hit shows as *South Pacific*, *The King and I*, *The Sound of Music* and *Oklahoma*.

**Freddie Mercury** *Died 24 November 1991* The Queen musical *We Will Rock You* continues to pack them in at theatres across the world, and re-releases of Queen classics fill the coffers of the Mercury estate.

## 20 People who found fame while still in their teens

**Boris Becker** was the youngest men's Wimbledon singles champion at the age of seventeen.

**Wilfred Benitez** in 1978 became an undisputed world boxing champion at the age of seventeen.

**Macaulay Culkin** was already established as a Hollywood star by the time he was thirteen, thanks to the *Home Alone* films.

**Leonardo DiCaprio** was eighteen when he beat four hundred other actors in auditions for a part opposite Robert De Niro in *This Boy's Life*. Within two years he was an established star in his own right.

**Judy Garland** was seventeen when *The Wizard of Oz* made her a worldwide movie star.

**Lady Jane Grey** was Queen of England for just over a week at the age of fifteen in 1553. She was executed a year later.

**George Harrison** was the youngest of The Beatles at nineteen when the Fab Four first started achieving global fame.

**Michael Jackson** was thirteen when he had his first solo hit song with 'Ben' but had already been a star for several years with the Jackson 5.

**Joan of Arc**, heroine of the Hundred Years War, was burned at the stake at nineteen.

**Nigel Kennedy** was established as a violin virtuoso in his early teens, as was his mentor Yehudi Menuhin.

**Olga Korbut**, a ballerina of the beams, was seventeen when she won gymnastic gold medals and hearts in the 1972 Olympics in Munich.

**Kylie Minogue** was eighteen and an established star in *Neighbours* when she recorded the first of a string of hit songs in 1987.

**Wolfgang Amadeus Mozart** was already an acclaimed composer by the time he entered his teens.

**Donny Osmond** was still in his teens when he emerged as the most popular of the singing family.

**Pelé** was a World Cup-winner with Brazil in Sweden in 1958 at the age of seventeen.

**Mickey Rooney** was a child star in Hollywood in the 1930s and stayed the course, marrying eight times along the way.

**Wayne Rooney** was the youngest ever player capped by England, and a multi-million-pound footballer while still in his teens.

**Shirley Temple**, the most famous of all the child Hollywood stars, was considered just about past it by the time she was thirteen.

**Stevie Wonder**, the blind singing keyboard player, has been a world star since his first hit song, 'Fingertips Pt 2', recorded at the age of thirteen.

**Tiger Woods** was the youngest ever US Amateur golf champion at the age of eighteen. It was just the start of his winning ways.

## 20 People born abroad who found fame in the USA

**Alexander Graham Bell** (Scotland)
**Irving Berlin** (Russia)
**Jim Carrey** (Canada)
**Andrew Carnegie** (Scotland)
**Errol Flynn** (Australia)
**Michael J. Fox** (Canada)
**Cary Grant** (England)
**Alfred Hitchcock** (England)
**Bob Hope** (England)
**Henry Kissinger** (Germany)
**John McEnroe** (Germany)
**Mike Myers** (Canada)
**Olivia Newton-John** (Australia)
**Leslie Nielsen** (Canada)
**Joseph Pulitzer** (Hungary)
**William Shatner** (Canada)
**Jerry Springer** (England)
**Elizabeth Taylor** (England)

**Rudolph Valentino** (Argentina)
**Bruce Willis** (Germany)

## 20 Famous left-handed celebrities

**Woody Allen**
**Pierce Brosnan**
**George Bush Snr**
**David Cameron**
**Glen Campbell**
**Bill Clinton**
**Phil Collins**
**Tom Cruise**
**Matt Dillon**
**Gerald Ford**
**Art Garfunkel**
**Uri Geller**
**Jimi Hendrix**
**Angelina Jolie**
**Lisa Kudrow**
**Paul McCartney**
**George Michael**
**Morrissey**
**Emma Thompson**
**Prince William**

## 30 Famous people who died before they were thirty

**Anne Frank**, posthumously famous for her extraordinary diary of a life spent in hiding, died in a Nazi concentration camp at fifteen

**Tutankhamun**, Egyptian pharaoh, died at eighteen

**Billy the Kid**, outlaw, gunned down at twenty

**Sid Vicious**, punk rocker, overdosed at twenty-one

**Stuart Sutcliffe**, artist and an original member of The Beatles, died of a brain haemorrhage at twenty-one

**Duncan Edwards**, England football international, victim of the Manchester United Munich air disaster at twenty-one

**Buddy Holly**, rock 'n' roll idol, died in a plane crash at twenty-two

**Lillian Board**, British Olympics heroine, died of cancer at twenty-two

**River Phoenix**, film star, overdosed at twenty-three

**James Dean**, American cult actor, died in a high-speed car crash at twenty-four

**Lee Harvey Oswald**, John F. Kennedy's alleged assassin, shot by Jack Ruby at twenty-four

**John Keats**, English poet, died of tuberculosis at twenty-five

**Wilfred Owen**, First World War poet, killed in the final month of the war at twenty-five

**Jean Harlow**, 1930s screen goddess, died of kidney failure at twenty-six

**Otis Redding**, American soul singer, died in a plane crash at twenty-six

**Ned Kelly**, Australian outlaw and folk hero, hanged at twenty-six

**Janis Joplin**, American rock singer, overdosed at twenty-seven

**Rupert Brooke**, English First World War poet, killed in action at twenty-seven

**Jimi Hendrix**, American rock guitarist and singer, choked on his vomit after an overdose at twenty-seven

**Brian Jones**, Rolling Stones guitarist, found dead in his swimming pool at twenty-seven

**Jim Morrison**, rock singer in The Doors, died of heart failure at twenty-seven

**Kurt Cobain,** lead singer of Nirvana, alleged to have shot himself at twenty-seven

**Jochen Rindt**, Formula One driver, died during a practice lap at twenty-eight

**Percy Bysshe Shelley**, English poet, drowned at twenty-nine

**Christopher Marlowe**, English poet and playwright, stabbed in mysterious circumstances at twenty-nine

**Anne Boleyn,** Henry VIII's second wife, beheaded at twenty-nine

**Marc Bolan**, British glam-rock singer, died in a car crash at twenty-nine

**Anne Brontë**, English novelist, died of tuberculosis at twenty-nine

**Mike Hawthorn**, British Formula One driver, died in a car crash at twenty-nine

**Hank Williams**, country singing idol, died of heart failure caused by alcoholism at twenty-nine

## 10 Famous people who overcame handicaps

**Homer**, blind creator of the *Iliad* and the *Odyssey*.

**Ludwig van Beethoven**, partly deaf from the age of thirty and totally deaf at forty-six – before he composed his greatest works.

**Horatio Nelson,** English naval hero despite losing an arm and an eye in battle.

**Sarah Bernhardt**, 'the Divine Sarah' of the French stage who continued to act after having a leg amputated.

**Douglas Bader**, Second World War pilot, who continued to fly in combat despite losing both legs.

**Louis Braille**, blind from the age of three, developed the Braille system of reading and writing for the blind.

**Helen Keller**, a prolific author and lecturer despite being blind and deaf.

**Joseph Pulitzer**, distinguished journalist, Congressman and Prize benefactor who was blind from the age of forty.

**Franklin D. Roosevelt**, paralysed by polio at the age of thirty-nine, before his first of four terms as United States President.

**Henri de Toulouse-Lautrec**, deformed after breaking both legs aged fourteen but became one of the great artists of the nineteenth century.

## Classical tales of the unexpected

**Wolfgang Amadeus Mozart** is one of the most famous composers of all time, but nobody knows where he is buried. His coffin lies in an unmarked pauper's grave in a cemetery in Vienna. The monument built in the cemetery has been positioned on the basis of an educated guess.

To stimulate his creative juices, **Beethoven** used to pour a jug of cold water over his head before sitting at the piano for a composing session.

**Johann Sebastian Bach**, who was totally blind in the last years of his life, fathered twenty children, ten of whom died in infancy.

German composer **Robert Schumann** suffered from schizophrenia and was convinced that imaginary friends were helping him with his compositions. They were at work in his head when he threw himself into the River Rhine. He was saved from drowning and spent his last days in a mental hospital, where he died at the age of forty-six.

Like Schumann, **Piotr Ilyich Tchaikovsky** tried to commit suicide. When his marriage was on the verge of collapse (because of his homosexuality), he was so depressed that he walked into the River Volga but was rescued and went on to write his greatest compositions – sponsored by posted payments from a lady he never met.

**Richard Wagner**, Hitler's favourite composer, shared his home amicably with his wife and two mistresses.

England's greatest classical composer **Edward Elgar** used to go for drives in his open-topped car accompanied by his three dogs. All four of them – Edward and the dogs – wore goggles. His journey often took him to Molineux to watch his favourite team Wolverhampton Wanderers play, and in 1898 he composed the first ever terrace chant: 'Malpass banged the leather for goal.'

**George Frederick Handel** challenged fellow composer **Johann Mattheson** to a duel in 1704 during a dispute as to which of them should play the harpsichord at an opera. They fought with swords, and only a large button on Handel's coat saved him from being run through.

**Luciano Pavarotti** received a record 165 curtains calls and applause lasting one hour seven minutes after singing the part of Nemorino in Donizetti's *L'Elisir d'Amore* at the Berlin Opera House in 1968.

Italian tenor **Enrico Caruso** was arrested in the Monkey House at New York Central Park in 1906 after a woman claimed he had molested her and pinched her bottom. At the end of one of the first major celebrity trials of the twentieth century, Enrico was found guilty and fined ten dollars. *The Great Caruso, my arse!*

## 20 Trivial anecdotes just for the record

**Irving Berlin**, one of the most prolific songwriters in history, could not read a note of music and, when composing, played the piano only in the

key of F sharp, using all the black keys. He had a special piano manufactured on which he could change key by pushing down a custom-built pedal.

British actor **Rupert Everett** sang backing vocals on the Madonna song 'American Pie' . . . **Michael Douglas** sang on the Billy Ocean song 'When the Going Gets Tough, the Tough Get Going' . . . **Tim Rice** was one of the backing singers on the Scaffold hit 'Lily the Pink'.

Self-taught **Buddy Holly** had an unconventional way of playing the guitar, using only down strokes with his plectrum. The 'correct' way is up and down, but it did not stop him pioneering rock 'n' roll with his group The Crickets, the first group to write and record their own music away from the clutches of the major recording companies.

Pop group **Dexy's Midnight Runners** (they had a No. 1 hit with 'Come On Eileen') appeared on *Top of the Pops* in 1982 singing their latest release 'Jackie Wilson Said'. Featured on a screen behind them as they played was a huge blown-up picture of Scottish darts player *Jocky* Wilson.

Infamous serial killer **Charles Manson** once auditioned for the 1960s group The Monkees. He was turned down.

**Paul McCartney** wanted to give his Shetland sheepdog Martha a present. So at the end of The Beatles song 'A Day in the Life' the studio engineers added an ultrasonic whistle that can be detected only by dogs.

**Brian Epstein**, manager of The Beatles in their peak years, was told by a Decca executive when he tried to get the group a recording contract: 'Go back to Liverpool, Mr Epstein. Take it from me, groups with guitars are out!'

**Olivia Newton-John** is the granddaughter of Max Born, German winner of the 1954 Nobel Prize for physics.

A worldwide count of **Elvis Presley** impersonators topped fifty thousand, including black Elvises, Native American Elvises, Chinese and Russian Elvises, Serbo-Croatian, Jewish and Tibetan Elvises, gay, dwarf (sorry, vertically challenged), handicapped, imprisoned, nude, skiing, snowboarding, surfing and skydiving Elvises . . . even Elvis elves. Strangest of all: a lesbian Elvis impersonator who calls herself Elvis Herselvis.

Monkee **Mike Nesmith**'s mother invented liquid-paper correction fluid for typists.

Explaining why he had selected Hercules as his middle name, **Elton John** said: 'I liked the name of the horse in one of my favourite sitcoms, *Steptoe and Son*. It was called Hercules, and I asked myself, "Am I hung like a horse?" The answer was unquestionably yes, so I gave myself the name because it was quite appropriate.'

Asked how much tennis meant to him, **Cliff Richard** said: 'If I'm in the middle of hitting a most fantastic cross-court backhand top spin and someone says, "Can you stop now and have sex," I'll say: "No thanks!"'

Englishman **John Stafford Smith** composed the music for the American national anthem, 'The Star Spangled Banner'.

The American-based composers of 'When Irish Eyes Are Smiling' never visited the Emerald Isle.

Country singer **Loretta Lynn** was married at twelve, had four children by the time she was seventeen, and was a grandmother at twenty-nine.

**Hank Williams** never read anything but kids' comics, yet established himself as a poet-lyricist whose work was admired by scholars and country fans alike.

Jamaican reggae legend **Bob Marley** was the son of a white sailor from Liverpool. The Mersey Beat got everywhere!

**Elvis Costello** is the son of former British big band singer Ross MacManus, who sang the 'I'm a secret lemonade drinker' jingle in the popular R. White's television commercials.

Both **Eric Clapton** and **Bobby Darin** grew up believing that their mothers were their older sisters.

**Mick Jagger** and The Rolling Stones were appearing on Ed Sullivan's prestigious coast-to-coast show when trying to make the breakthrough in the United States in the 1960s. Also on the show was a choir of forty-four nuns. The show's host listened to The Stones rehearsing their song, 'Let's Spend the Night Together'. Sullivan, on whose show Elvis Presley had famously been shot only from the waist up, nearly had a fit. An ultimatum was given to Mick: 'Instead of spending "the night together" make it "spend some time together".' Mick wanted to walk off, but realised the importance of the show as publicity for the band. When he sang the new lyrics he rolled his eyes to the camera each time he came to the amended words. Nobody was left in any doubt what he thought of the censorship.

# The final curtain, you wouldn't believe it!

And so to (almost) the final list. This is a scattergun collection that goes across the board to find 'you wouldn't believe it' facts about a wide range of celebrities. There are a lot of weird people out there!

**Orville Wright**, who with his brother Wilbur pioneered powered flight, numbered the eggs that his chickens produced so he could eat them in the order they were laid.

Telephone inventor **Alexander Graham Bell** never phoned his wife or mother because both were deaf.

**Leonardo da Vinci** could write with one hand and draw with the other simultaneously.

Swedish confectionery maker **Roland Ohisson** was buried in a coffin made entirely of chocolate.

Prussian Field Marshal **Gebhard von Blücher** – who played a key role in helping Wellington defeat Napoleon at the Battle of Waterloo – later thought he was pregnant with an elephant . . . and that the father was a French soldier!

**Attila the Hun** – one of the most feared military men in history and a survivor of many a fierce battle – died on his wedding night while trying to consummate his marriage.

**Alexander the Great**, **Julius Caesar**, **Napoleon Bonaparte** and **Benito Mussolini** all had a morbid fear of cats.

Revolutionary **Ho Chi Minh** once worked as a pastry cook in the kitchen of the prestigious Carlton Hotel in London . . . **Lenin** lived in London, where he had secret planning meetings with **Leon Trotsky** . . . and **Karl Marx** spent his last years in London and is buried at Highgate Cemetery.

**Adolf Hitler** was voted *Time* magazine's Man of the Year in 1938, a year before the start of the Second World War. Russian leader **Josef Stalin** got the vote in 1939, and **Winston Churchill** in 1940.

**Josef Stalin** stood 5ft 6in tall, **Adolf Hitler** 5ft 8in, **Winston Churchill** 5ft 6in and General **Charles DeGaulle** 6ft 4in. **Napoleon Bonaparte** was reported to have been 5ft 5in.

**Stalin** had webbed toes on his left foot . . . **Josef Goebbels** had a club foot . . . **Hermann Goering** was a drug addict hooked on morphine.

**Maximilien Robespierre**, the French revolutionary leader who sent thousands to the guillotine during the Reign of Terror, could not stand the sight of blood. He himself was guillotined.

**Al Capone** used to hand out calling cards describing himself as a used furniture dealer. Wonder if he made them a sofa they couldn't refuse?

Famous historic epileptics include **Julius Caesar**, **Vincent van Gogh**, **Napoleon Bonaparte**, **Alfred Nobel**, **Lord Byron**, **Alexander the Great**, **Joan of Arc** and **Lenin**.

**Van Gogh** sold only one of his paintings throughout his life (*The Red Vineyard*). He produced all his work – 900 paintings and 1100 drawings – in the last ten years of his life before he committed suicide in 1890. One hundred years after his death his portrait of *Doctor Gachet* was sold for a record forty-six million pounds.

Chinese leader **Mao Tse-tung** never once brushed his teeth. He used to rinse them with green tea. His logic: 'A tiger never brushes its teeth.'

**Mata Hari**, executed by a firing squad as a German spy during the First World War, sounded like an exotic Oriental. She was in fact a Dutch divorcee called Margaretha McLeod (née Zeller), who had left her alcoholic Scottish husband to follow a career as an exotic dancer.

We all know that Frenchman **Louis Blériot** was the first man to fly across the English Channel in 1909. But did you know that New York journalist **Harriet Quimby** was the first woman to achieve it in 1912, flying a monoplane loaned to her by Blériot? Three months later she became one of the first women to die in a plane crash.

Some history books suggest that the condom was named after a Dr Condom, who invented it to stop **King Charles II** from breeding illegitimate children who could have laid claim to the throne. I think that's a load of old cock.

According to some historians, the following famous people died of syphilis-related illnesses: **Alexander the Great**, **Christopher Columbus**, **Henry VIII**, **Lenin**, **Lord Randolph Churchill** (father of Winston), **Oscar Wilde** and **Al Capone**.

**Queen Anne**, last of the Stuart monarchs, had seventeen children but none outlived her. All but one died in infancy.

Fashion designer **Ralph Lauren** changed his name from Lipschitz. Spoilsport. Imagine saying to a woman: 'That's a lovely Lipschitz you're wearing.'

**Oliver Cromwell** was exhumed two years after his death and then hung, drawn and quartered.

**Florence Nightingale** spent her life nursing others, but in her later years became a hypochondriac who took to her bed for months because she was convinced she was dying. Eventually, she was proved right.

In 1939 author **Ernest Vincent Wright** had a 50,000-word novel published that did not include a single letter 'e', the most common vowel in the English language. It meant not one use of the definite article. He jammed down the 'e' on his typewriter to make sure one did not slip in by mistake. Californian Wright was sixty-seven when he wrote the book in just 165 days. 'I just fancied the challenge,' he said. To give you a taste, this was his first paragraph:

> If youth, throughout all history, had had a champion to stand up for it; to show a doubting world that a child can think; and, possibly, do it practically; you wouldn't constantly run across folks today who claim that 'a child don't know anything'. A child's brain starts functioning at birth; and has, amongst its many infant convolutions, thousands of dormant atoms, into which God has put a mystic possibility for noticing an adult's act, and figuring out its purport.

Articles written without using a specific letter are known as lipograms. Man-of-all-parts **Gyles Brandreth** is one of Britain's foremost exponents. He specialises in dropping a different letter from each of Shakespeare's plays. All 'i's were excluded from *Hamlet*, so the famous soliloquy became: 'To be or not to be; that's the query'. He also rewrote *Twelfth Night* without the letters 'l' and 'o', *Othello* without any 'o's, and *Macbeth* without any 'a's or 'e's. Macbeth, my bottom!

German physicist Professor Phillip Lenard suffered from onomatophobia . . . a fear of specific names. He could, for instance, not utter or hear **Sir Isaac Newton** without going into a fit. When he needed to use the name in a lecture, he would turn his back on his students while a member of the class would mime Newton's name.

Hollywood stars **Lana Turner**, **Mickey Rooney**, **Zsa Zsa Gabor**, **Stan Laurel** and **Georgia Holt** – Cher's mother – each married eight times. Holt

got hitched to John Sarkisian – Cher's dad – three times, and Stan Laurel had a hat-trick of marriages to Virginia Rogers.

A spectacular feature of *The Wizard of Oz*, which propelled **Judy Garland** to global fame, was the tornado that swept across the Kansas skies. The day Judy died of an overdose in London in 1969 a tornado ripped across Kansas.

**Bing Crosby** and **Clark Gable** both had their stick-out ears pinned back with gum in their early film appearances.

French actress **Sarah Bernhardt** went to great lengths to get herself and her plays publicised. Sarah, who had a leg amputated late in her career, once toured with a huge, silk-lined coffin permanently at the side of the stage, sleeping in it and entertaining some of her string of lovers to what can only be described as a (false) leg over!

**Clara Bow** – the 'It Girl' of 1920s Hollywood – was famously alleged to have 'taken on' every member of the University of Southern California football team in a wild night of debauchery in Los Angeles. Included in the team was Marion Morrison, later to become famous as **John Wayne**. I think the story has been invented, though, otherwise she would have been Clara Bow-legged.

In the greatest Hollywood publicity stunt ever, producer **David O. Selznick** auditioned 1400 actresses for the part of Scarlett O'Hara in *Gone with the Wind*. He had decided to give the role to Vivien Leigh a year before the interviews started.

**Vivien Leigh** hated kissing co-star **Clark Gable** in rehearsals for *Gone with the Wind* – because 'he had excessively bad breath'. Frankly, my dear, she did give a damn. Mind you, it could have been worse. The part of Rhett could have been played by Mao Tse-tung.

Hollywood glamour actress **Kim Basinger** suffered so badly from agoraphobia when she was young that she could not leave her home for six months, and needed psychological help to conquer her affliction.

There is plenty of evidence of a curse on any actor playing the part of Superman. **Kirk Alyn**, the man of steel in the 1940s television series, developed Alzheimer's disease . . . **George Reeves**, 1950s TV Superman, shot himself in 1959 . . . **Clayton 'Bud' Collyer**, radio and cartoon voice of Clark Kent, died early of a circulatory ailment . . . while **Christopher Reeve**, most famous of the screen Supermen, was paralysed from the neck down in a horseriding accident.

President **Jimmy Carter** watched nearly five hundred Hollywood films during his four years in the White House.

President **Ronald Reagan** used the private White House cinema like a Hollywood movie theatre, getting through several bowlfuls of popcorn while watching newly released films. He rarely viewed the old black-and-white movies in which he starred. What a good judge.

**David Rice Atchinson** served as the twelfth President of the United States . . . for exactly one day. His predecessor James Polk left office on a Saturday, and the new President Zachary Taylor could not take the Oath until the following Monday. The United States' rules of succession meant that Rice – as leader of the Senate – had to stand in. It has been claimed that he was the only President who during his term of office neither raised taxes nor started a war.

Outrageous singer **Ozzy Osbourne** worked hard at developing his image as the 'Prince of Darkness'. MTV publicists described him while advertising the fly-on-the-wall series *The Osbournes* as 'America's favourite father'. Osbourne's reaction? In his thick Midlands accent: 'Well, f*** me!'

Ozzy Osbourne, named America's favourite father. Not the best image for the old Prince of Darkness! Perhaps he's seen the f***ing light.

**Paul Newman** took a grilling from the critics following his first starring role in *The Silver Chalice*, in which he played a Greek slave. One reviewer said that he delivered his lines 'with the sincerity and emotion of a Pullman conductor announcing the next stop'. Newman was so disappointed with his performance that he took out a full-page advertisement in the trade paper *Variety* apologising for it. Lorne Greene made his screen debut in the same turkey of a film. In his next movie, *Somebody up There Likes Me*, Newman was hailed as 'even better than Brando'.

The great **Nijinsky**, one of the most famous and fêted ballet dancers of all time, became paranoid in his mid-twenties, convinced that a former male lover was out to wreck his career by leaving a stage trapdoor open. He danced his last role at the age of just twenty-seven, and spent the rest of his life getting psychiatric treatment.

The film title the *The Madness of George III* was changed to plain *The Madness of King George* because it was decided that the average American moviegoer would consider it the third in a series of films, and would not bother to go to see it because they had missed the first two.

When he was Governor of Georgia, **Jimmy Carter** reported that he had seen a UFO. This was not publicised until his successful presidential campaign several years later, when he told reporters: 'It was the darndest thing I've ever seen. It was big, it was very bright, it changed colours and it was about the size of the moon. We watched it for ten minutes, but none of us could figure out what it was. One thing's for sure, I'll never make fun of people who say they've seen unidentified objects in the sky. If I become President, I'll make every piece of information this country has about UFO sightings available to the public and the scientists.'

**Albert Einstein** might have devised the Theory of Relativity, but he couldn't drive a car.

**Tom Hanks** is the yo-yo man of Hollywood. He put on thirty pounds for his part in *A League of Their Own*, lost thirty pounds to play an AIDS victim in *Philadelphia*, and then gained fifty pounds for his role in *Cast Away*, before shedding it during the shooting of the film.

When engaged to Winona Ryder, **Johnny Depp** had 'Winona forever' tattooed on his arm. After they broke up, he had the 'n' and the 'a' surgically removed so it now reads, 'Wino forever'!

And finally . . .

## 10 Actors who have shown their bare bum on the screen

**Marlon Brando** (*Last Tango in Paris*)
**Robert Carlyle** (*The Full Monty*)
**John Cleese** (*A Fish Called Wanda*)
**Richard Gere** (*American Gigolo*)
**Harvey Keitel** (*The Piano*)
**Heath Ledger** (*Brokeback Mountain*)
**Ewan McGregor** (*Young Adam*)
**Geoffrey Rush** (*Quills*)
**Arnold Schwarzenegger** (*Terminator*)
**Bruce Willis** (*Colour of Night*)

Oh yes, and I flashed my bum as England manager Mike Bassett. Celebrities, my arse!

# You've gotta laugh

Ken Dodd is playing for charity on *Who Wants to Be a Millionaire* and has reached the £1 million question.

Chris Tarrant says, 'Right, Ken, this is for one million pounds, and remember, you still have two lifelines left, so please take your time.'

Ken takes a deep breath, and then watches the screen, waiting for his vital question to come up.

You can cut the atmosphere with a knife as Tarrant reads the question from his computer: 'For one million pounds, what type of animal lives in a sett?'

He then reads the four choices: 'Is it a) a badger; b) a ferret; c) a mole or d) a cuckoo?'

Ken ponders for a while and says, 'No, I'm sorry, Chris, I'm not too sure. I'll have to go fifty–fifty.'

'Right, Ken, let's take away two wrong answers and see what you're left with.'

'Ferret' and 'mole' disappear from the screen, leaving 'Badger' and 'Cuckoo'.

Ken has a long think, then scratches his head and says: 'No, Chris, I'm still not sure, I'm going to have to phone a friend.'

'So who are you going to call, Ken?' says Chris.

'Hmmm, I think I'll call my fellow Scouser Stan Boardman.'

So a call is put through to Stan at his home.

'Stan, this is Chris Tarrant from *Who Wants to Be a Millionaire*. I've got your pal Ken Dodd here, and with your

help he could win one million pounds for his favourite charity. The next voice you hear will be Ken's. There are only two choices for the answer, and you have thirty seconds to answer.'

'Bring it on,' says Stan.

'Hello Stanley,' says Ken. 'Doddy here. What type of animal lives in a sett? Is it a badger or a cuckoo?'

'It's a badger, Doddy,' says Stan without a moment's hesitation.

'You sure, Stanley?' says Ken. 'There is a lot riding on this. I don't want to get it wrong.'

'Definitely, Doddy,' Stan stresses. 'One hundred per cent. It's a badger. No doubt whatsoever.'

'Right, Chris,' says Ken, 'I'll go with Stanley. The answer's badger.'

'Final answer, Ken?'

'Final answer, Chris.'

'That's the correct answer. You've won one million pounds for your charity!'

'That's tatifilarious,' says Ken. 'Well done, Stan Boardman. The man's a genius.'

After the show, Ken phones Stan to thank him.

'Stanley, that was brilliant. I thought I might be taking a gamble giving you a call, but you played a blinder! How the heck did you know that a badger lives in a sett?'

'Oh, I didn't, Ken,' replies Stan. 'But everybody knows a cuckoo lives in a clock!'